Office 2010

VISUAL™

Quick Steps

Visual

John Wiley & Sons, Inc.

Office 2010 Visual™ Quick Steps

Published by
John Wiley & Sons, Inc.
10475 Crosspoint Boulevard
Indianapolis, IN 46256
www.wiley.com

Published simultaneously in Canada

Copyright © 2012 by John Wiley & Sons, Inc., Indianapolis, Indiana

ISBN: 978-1-118-33877-3

Manufactured in the United States of America

10 9 8 7 6 5 4 3 2 1

Trademark Acknowledgments

Contact Us

For general information on our other products and services or to obtain technical support, please contact our Customer Care Department within the U.S. at (877) 762-2974, outside the U.S. at (317) 572-3993 or fax (317) 572-4002.

For technical support please visit www.wiley.com/techsupport.

Disclaimer

In order to get this information to you in a timely manner, this book was based on a pre-release version of Microsoft Office 2010. There may be some minor changes between the screenshots in this book and what you see on your desktop. As always, Microsoft has the final word on how programs look and function; if you have any questions or see any discrepancies, consult the online help for further information about the software. For purposes of illustrating the concepts and techniques described in this book, the author has created various names, company names, mailing, e-mail, and Internet addresses, phone and fax numbers, and similar information, all of which are fictitious. Any resemblance of the fictitious names, addresses, phone and fax numbers, and similar information to any actual person, company and/or organization is unintentional and purely coincidental.

John Wiley & Sons, Inc.

Sales

Contact Wiley
at (877) 762-2974 or
fax (317) 572-4002.

Credits

Executive Editor
Jody Lefevere

Sr. Project Editor
Sarah Hellert

Technical Editor
Joyce Nielsen

Copy Editor
Scott Tullis

Editorial Director
Robyn Siesky

Business Manager
Amy Knies

Sr. Marketing Manager
Sandy Smith

Vice President and Executive Group Publisher
Richard Swadley

Vice President and Executive Publisher
Barry Pruett

Sr. Project Coordinator
Kristie Rees

Proofreader
Susan Hobbs

Screen Artists
Ana Carrillo
Jill A. Proll

Table of Contents

chapter 1   General Office 2010 Maximizing Tips

chapter 2   Timesaving Tips for Office Files

chapter 3   Boosting Your Productivity in Word

chapter **4** Utilizing Word's Document Building Tools

chapter **5** Optimizing Excel

Table of Contents

chapter 6 Polishing Your Spreadsheet Data

chapter 7 Increasing PowerPoint's Potential

chapter 8 Enhancing Your Presentations

General Office 2010 Maximizing Tips

The various applications in Microsoft Office 2010 — in particular, Word, Excel, and PowerPoint — share a common look and feel. Indeed, you can find many of the same features in each program, such as the Ribbon feature, the Quick Access toolbar, various program window controls, and the File tab.

This common look and feel is helpful when you perform certain tasks within Office applications. For example, creating a new document in Word is similar to creating a new document in Excel. The same goes for more complicated tasks, such as encrypting documents, tracking changes to a document, adding a digital signature, marking a document as final, and so on. This commonality makes mastering Office 2010 a snap.

This chapter focuses on tasks that transcend applications. That is, these tasks can be performed in more than one Office program.

Quick Steps

Customize the Quick Access Toolbar

Located in the top left corner of the program window sits the often underutilized Quick Access toolbar. The Quick Access toolbar provides easy access to often-used commands such as Save and Undo. In fact, it starts out with just a few default buttons. You can customize the Quick Access toolbar to change what commands are available and essentially make the toolbar into something that works for you.

Office enables you to add commands to the Quick Access toolbar three different ways. One is to select the desired command from the Customize Quick Access Toolbar menu. The menu only lists a few of the popular commands

and displays check marks next to each button that is actively in the toolbar. You can choose which of the common commands you want to display or hide.

Another way to add commands is to use the program's Options dialog box. You can simply right-click the command you want to add in the Ribbon and click Add to Quick Access Toolbar.

In addition to adding commands to the Quick Access toolbar, you can also move it from its default spot above the Ribbon to a spot below the Ribbon. To do so, click the arrow in the Quick Access toolbar and click Show Below the Ribbon from the menu that appears.

---

① Click the arrow to the right of the Quick Access toolbar.

Office displays the Customize Quick Access Toolbar menu.

② Click the command you want to add to the toolbar.

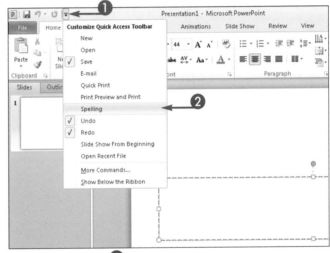

● A button for the selected command appears on the toolbar.

In this example, the Spelling button was added.

③ If you do not find the command you want to add, display the Customize Quick Access Toolbar menu again.

④ Click More Commands.

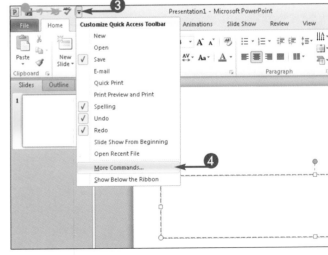

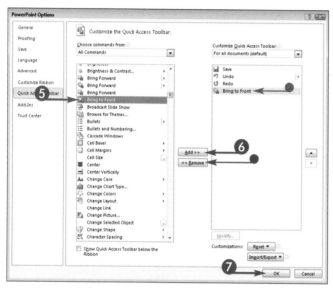

The program's Options dialog box opens with Quick Access toolbar options displayed.

⑤ In the left pane, click the command you want to add.

Note: If the command you want to add is not shown, click the Choose Commands From drop-down arrow and select All Commands.

⑥ Click Add.

● The command is added to the window's right list pane.

● To remove a command you do not want on the toolbar, click the command and click Remove.

⑦ Click OK to exit the dialog box.

● The Office program adds the new button to the toolbar.

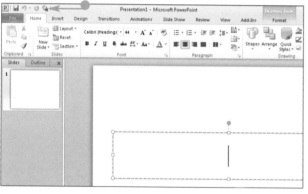

TIPS

Did You Know?

You can add groups of commands in the Ribbon to the Quick Access toolbar. To do so, right-click the group name in the Ribbon and click Add to Quick Access Toolbar. The group is stored under a single button; click the button to reveal the available commands in the group.

Customize It!

You may want the customized toolbar for use with the current document only. In the program's Options dialog box with the Quick Access Toolbar settings showing, you can specify whether you want the customized toolbar available for all documents or just the current one you are working on. Click the Customize Quick Access Toolbar drop-down arrow located over the right pane listing all the buttons you have added and choose an option. In PowerPoint, for example, you can customize the toolbar for the current presentation, or in Word, you can apply toolbar to the current document. The exact wording of the option varies based on what Office program you are using.

Customize the Ribbon

In Office 2010, the Ribbon is back and better than ever. The Office 2010 suite now offers a Ribbon of tools in every program. Designed to enable you to find the command necessary to complete a task more quickly and more intuitively than the menus and toolbars of old, the Ribbon is the go-to spot for accessing commands.

The Ribbon groups related commands together, placing them under clickable tabs. Each tab pertains to a certain type of task, such as formatting text, inserting items into a

document, laying out a page, reviewing a document, and so on. The tabs shown depend on what Office program is open, and what type of task is being performed.

You will be happy to know you can retool the Ribbon to suit the way you work in an Office program. You can add your own tab and populate it with buttons for not-so-common commands, add new groups to existing tabs, and reorder the tabs in the Ribbon. All buttons you add to a tab are organized into groups.

1. Right-click an empty area of the Ribbon.

   Office displays a context menu.

2. Click Customize the Ribbon.

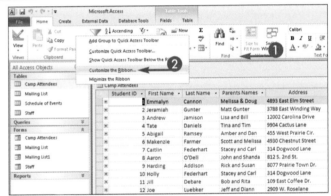

The program's Options dialog box opens with Ribbon options displayed.

3. Click New Tab.

   ● A new unnamed tab and group are added to the list.

4. With the new tab selected, click the Rename button to give the new tab a distinctive name.

   Note: *You can also rename any groups you add to the new tab; click the group name and click the Rename button.*

   The Rename dialog box opens.

5. Type a new name and click OK.

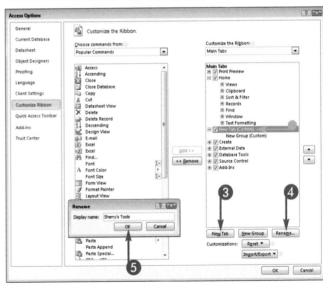

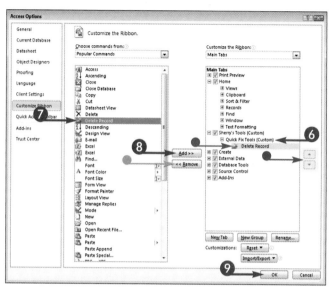

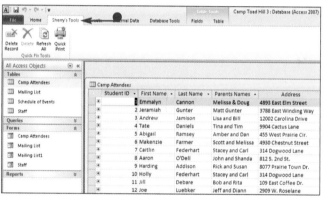

6 Click the new group name to select the group.

7 In the window's left pane, click a command you want to add to the new tab and group.

Note: *If the command you want to add is not shown, click the Choose Commands From drop-down arrow and select All Commands.*

8 Click Add.

● The command is added to window's right pane.

● You can use the Move Up and Move Down buttons to reposition a tab in the Ribbon, or reposition button order within a group or reposition groups within a tab.

● To remove a command, select it in the right pane and click Remove.

9 Click OK to exit the dialog box.

● The Office program adds the new tab and buttons to the Ribbon.

TIPS

Reverse It!

If you ever want to revert back to the original default Ribbon, open the program's Options dialog box and click the Reset button and choose whether you want to restore a single customized tab or all the customizations. If you choose the latter option, a prompt box opens and asks if you really want to delete all Ribbon and Quick Access Toolbar customizations. Click Yes to complete the process.

Did You Know?

Another way to open the program's Options dialog box is through the File tab. Click the File tab on the Ribbon, and then click Options. The nice thing about using the right-click method to open the dialog box is that it displays the Customize Ribbon settings automatically for you. If you use the File tab to open the dialog box, it displays the last set of options you edited.

Control the Ribbon Display

The Ribbon feature in Office 2010 is docked at the top of the program window where you can easily access all the many commands and features it offers. This location seems practical and efficient, but there may be times when the Ribbon is simply in the way. For example, you may want to view more of the document window you are working on. Although you cannot permanently remove the Ribbon, move it, or turn it off like you used to do with toolbars in Office 2003 and earlier, you can minimize it to get it out of the way. Anytime you need to utilize the commands again, you can summon the Ribbon back for display.

You can use two techniques to quickly minimize and summon the Ribbon. You can use the button located on the Ribbon itself, or you can right-click to display a context menu. Regardless of which method you employ, the Ribbon is significantly reduced in size, displaying only the tab names. This makes it extremely easy to bring the full Ribbon back again; just click a tab name.

Control the Ribbon with the Arrow Button

① Click the arrow button located next to the Help icon at the far right end of the Ribbon.

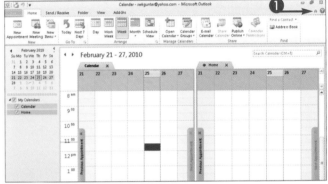

The Ribbon is minimized.

● Notice that the Ribbon's tabs are still present; to reveal options in a tab, click it; to hide them again, click the tab a second time.

② Click the arrow button again to redisplay the Ribbon.

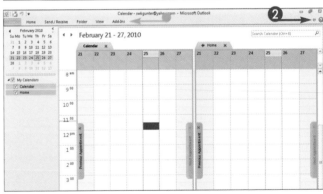

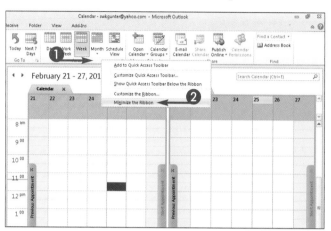

Control the Ribbon with the Context Menu

① Right-click an empty area of the Ribbon.

A context menu appears.

② Click Minimize the Ribbon.

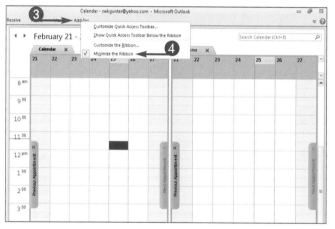

The Ribbon is minimized.

③ Right-click a tab name.

④ Click Minimize the Ribbon to remove the check mark from the command and restore the Ribbon display.

Did You Know?

Once you minimize the Ribbon, it stays that way even after you activate it to use a command. As soon as you finish the task at hand and move the mouse pointer off the Ribbon, it is minimized again automatically. To turn this minimizing effect off, click the arrow button (⌃) at the end of the Ribbon.

Customize It!

If Microsoft's order of tabs on the Ribbon does not fit into your left-handed style, you can move the tabs around on the Ribbon to better work for your personal usage. In the Options dialog box for customizing a Ribbon, you can use the Move Up and Move Down buttons (▲ and ▼) to change the order of tabs or of groups and commands. See the previous task, "Customize the Ribbon," to learn more.

Automate Office Tasks with Macros

If you frequently use an Office program to complete the same task — for example, to format the cells in a spreadsheet a certain way, or to insert a table in a Word document that contains a certain number of rows and columns — you can expedite the process by recording a macro. When you record a macro, you essentially record a series of actions; then you can run the macro you recorded to automatically perform the recorded actions.

One way to access the controls for recording a macro is from the Developer tab on the Ribbon. This tab is not shown by default, however. To display the Developer tab, right-click an empty area of the Ribbon and click Customize the Ribbon to open the Options dialog box. Click the Developer tab check box in the right pane to turn the tab on. Click OK and you are ready to record your own macros.

① Click the Developer tab in the Ribbon.

② In the Code group, click Record Macro.

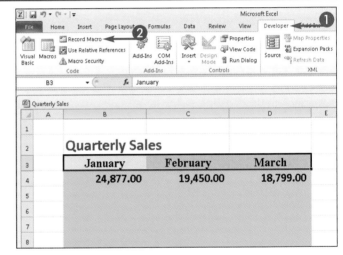

The Record Macro dialog box opens.

③ Type a name for the macro.

Note: *No spaces are allowed in macro names.*

④ Click here and select the template(s) in which you want the macro to be available.

⑤ Type a description of the macro.

⑥ Click OK.

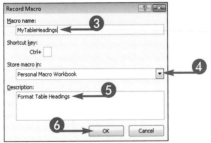

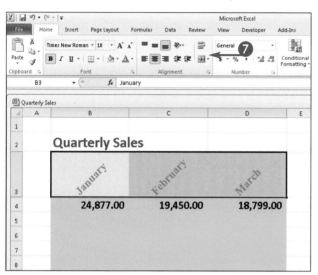

⑦ Perform the actions you want to record.

This example formats a series of headings.

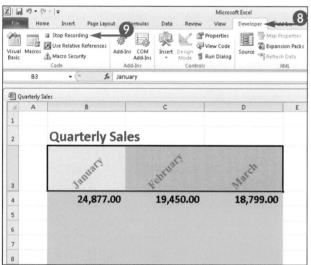

⑧ Click the Developer tab.

⑨ Click Stop Recording.

The application saves the macro.

TIPS

Apply It!

To run a macro you have recorded, click the Developer tab and click Macros in the Code group. In the Macros dialog box that appears, click the macro you want to run, and then click Run.

Caution!

Because macros can be created for malicious purposes, they are often disabled by default. To enable the use of macros in a particular document, click the File tab, click the Options button, click Trust Center, click Trust Center Settings, and then click Macro Settings. Finally, click Disable All Macros with Notification (◉ changes to ◯). That way, when Office encounters a document that contains macros, it displays a security dialog box that enables you to specify whether the macros should be allowed.

Change the Default Font and Size

You can control the font and size that Office automatically applies to every Word document or Excel workbook you open. By default, both programs apply a pre-set font and size to every new document or workbook you create. These settings are in place and ready to go so you can start entering data right away. You can certainly apply formatting to change the font and size as you add data, but if you use the same font and size for every file you create, why not instruct the program to assign those settings at startup?

In Word, you use the Font dialog box to assign new default settings. In Excel, you use the Excel Options dialog box to assign a new default font and size. PowerPoint does not utilize default sizes.

Once you specify new default settings, those settings are in place for any new files you create.

Change Word's Default Font

① Click the dialog box launcher in the Font group on the Home tab.

Note: Many of the tool groups in the Office Ribbons have icons in the corners you can click to open associated dialog boxes. In this example, the icon in the Font group, also called the Font dialog box launcher, opens the Font dialog box.

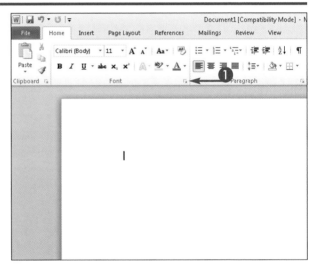

The Font dialog box opens.

② Select a new font and size from the available settings.

③ Click Set As Default.

A prompt box appears asking you whether you want the settings to apply to the current document or all documents.

④ Make your selection and click OK to apply the new settings.

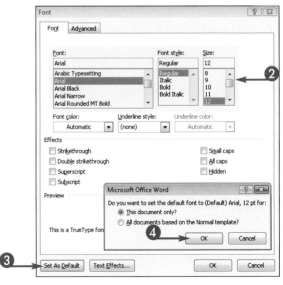

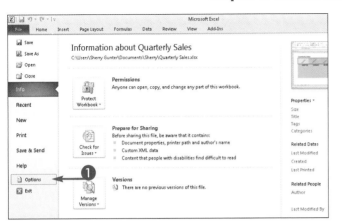

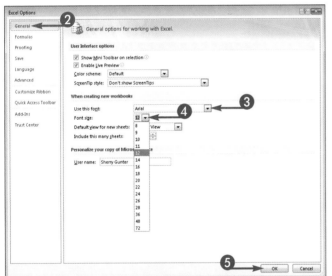

Change Excel's Default Font

① Click the File tab and click Options.

The Excel Options dialog box opens.

② Click General if it is not already shown.

③ Click the Use This Font drop-down arrow and choose another font.

④ Click the Font Size drop-down arrow and choose another size.

⑤ Click OK.

The new settings are assigned.

More Options!

Speaking of fonts, Word 2010 now supports OpenType ligatures. *Ligatures* refer to typography characters whose shape depends on surrounding characters, such as the letter f combined with the letter l or i. OpenType is a format for scalable fonts. OpenType ligatures are not enabled by default. To turn them on, open the Font dialog box by clicking the dialog box launcher in the Font group on the Home tab of the Ribbon. Click the Advanced tab and select a ligature from the OpenType features. Click OK to exit the dialog box and apply the new setting.

Timesaving Tips for Office Files

Office files come in several different "flavors" depending on the program. In Word, files you create are referred to as *documents*, but in Excel, they are called *workbooks*. In PowerPoint, files are *presentations*. Regardless of the official name, an Office file is simply the stored data you save in a program.

Because files are such a basic part of using an application, they share a lot of the same elements and tasks. For example, Word, Excel, and PowerPoint share a similar Save As dialog box from which you control the file name, format type, and storage location. The Office programs also share a similar-looking Open dialog box from which you choose what file you want to open.

There are lots of other things you can do with your files besides just save them and open them again. For example, in Word, Excel, and PowerPoint you can control the default Save location for your files. If you always save your files to a particular work folder, for example, you can add the folder's path to the program so it saves files to that location by default, unless you direct otherwise.

You can also activate security features, save files as PDF documents, and more.

This chapter shows you several different tasks that apply to Office files. Office 2010 has retooled the old Office button (introduced in Office 2007) into a File tab on the Ribbon that, when clicked, displays a whole screen full of options for working with your files, so make it your first stop in seeing what sort of tasks you can perform on or with your Office files.

Quick Steps

Change the Default File Save Location

You can tell Microsoft Office programs where you want to store files you create. Ordinarily, when you open the Save As dialog box to save your files in Word, Excel, and PowerPoint, these programs select the Documents folder as the default working folder for storage. You may prefer to use a different destination folder. For example, you may have a work folder set up to hold all the Excel workbooks you create. Instead of manually selecting a different folder from the dialog box each time you save, you can tell the Office program to list a default folder instead. This can save you some time and effort when saving your files.

You can control the default file location through the Office program's Options dialog box. For Word, Excel, and PowerPoint, the default file location is listed under the Save options.

When specifying a new default folder, you can type the full path to the folder. In Word you can also use the Browse button to navigate to the destination folder. A folder path includes the drive label and any hierarchical folders the destination folder is listed under, such as C:\Users\Bob\Work Stuff.

① Click File.

② Click Options.

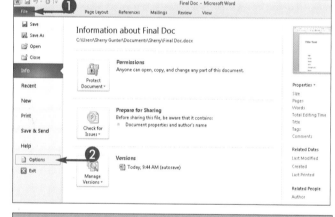

The program's Options dialog box opens.

③ Click the Save tab.

④ In Word, click the Browse button next to the Default file location box.

In Excel and PowerPoint, you must type in the full folder path. You can triple-click inside the Default File Location box to select the existing text and type the new path.

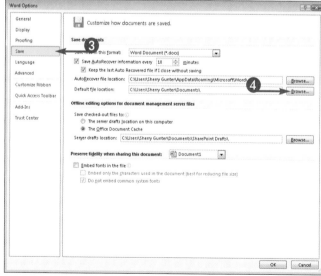

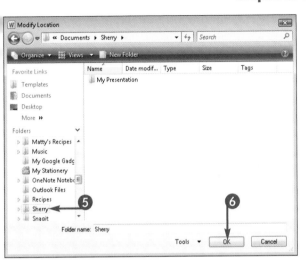

⑤ Navigate to the folder you want to use.

⑥ Click OK.

⑦ Click OK to exit the Options dialog box and apply the new setting.

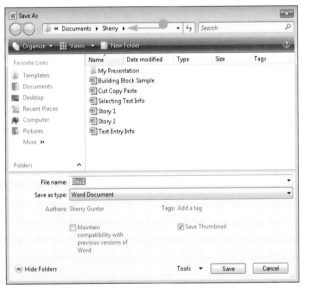

● The next time you use the Save As dialog box, the specified folder appears listed by default.

Customize It!

You can also specify a default file format to save to each time you save an Office file. Each Office program saves to a particular file type. For example, Word automatically saves documents as a Word Document file type (.docx) unless you choose otherwise. You may want to save all your documents as plain text files (.txt) or Microsoft Works files (.wps). You can set a different file type as the default type to save yourself a step. For Word, Excel, or PowerPoint, open the program's Options dialog box and click the Save tab. Display the Save Files in This Format drop-down menu and choose a different file format.

Save Office Files as PDF Documents

Saving files as PDF documents is one way to keep a file's content intact without requiring the recipient to have a copy of Office 2010 installed on his or her computer. PDF (Portable Document Format) is a popular file format from Adobe for sharing documents just as they were intended to be viewed, including all the content, formatting, and page layout elements. In essence, the PDF format captures all the elements of a document much like an electronic image that you can view, navigate, and print. Anyone can open a PDF file using the free Adobe Acrobat Reader software. PDF files are ideal for sharing on the Internet, easy to print using professional printer services, and the PDF open standard lets users share files regardless of

what program or platform was used to create the file. In previous versions of Office, you needed an add-in to convert documents. Office 2010 includes a built-in PDF writer to help you save your files to the PDF format.

When creating a PDF document, you have the option of creating an XPS document. Microsoft's own version of PDF-like documents are XML documents, commonly called XPS, short for XML Paper Specification. Like the PDF format, XPS documents include information defining the document's layout, appearance, and printing information. Unlike PDFs, however, XPS documents can be opened only by Windows XP, Vista, or Windows 7 users.

① Click File.

② Click Save & Send.

③ Click Create PDF/XPS Document.

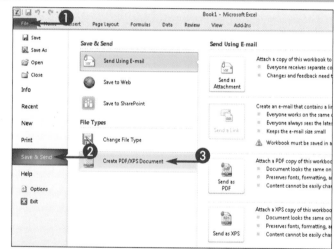

④ Click Create a PDF/XPS.

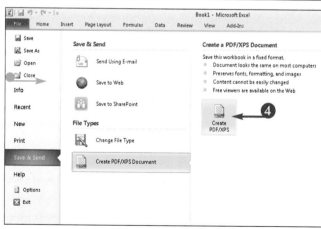

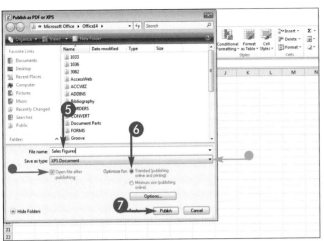

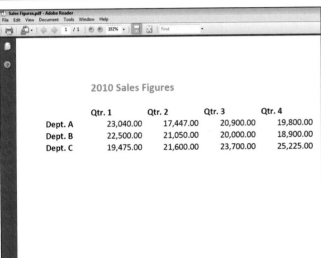

The program's Publish as PDF or XPS dialog box opens with the PDF file format selected by default.

⑤ Type a name for the file.

● To change the file type to PDF or XPS, click here and choose the correct file type.

⑥ Click an optimizing option (◎ changes to ◉). Choose Standard for printing, or Minimum size for online publishing.

● If you want to open the document in a PDF or XPS viewer after saving, leave this check box selected.

⑦ Click Publish.

The PDF document opens in the Adobe Reader window. If it is an XPS document, it opens in an XPS viewer.

More Options!

For more publishing options for PDF files, click the Options button in the Publish as PDF or XPS dialog box. This opens the Options dialog box where you find controls for setting the page range, choosing what items are published, and what nonprinting information is included. Click OK to apply any changes.

Did You Know?

You can also save your Office files as Web pages. In the Save As dialog box, click the Save as Type drop-down arrow and select either Single File Web Page or Web Page. The Single File Web Page option creates a single document without any supporting files for graphics and other elements. The Web Page option creates a folder for supporting elements along with the HTML file.

Remove Sensitive Document Information

If you plan to share an Office document with others, whether via e-mail or by some other method, you might want to first ensure that the document is void of personal, company, or other private information that may be stored in the document's metadata or in the document itself.

This information might include comments, tracked changes, or annotations; information about the document's author, status, category, keywords, and so on; hidden information (such as text, rows, columns, worksheets, or what have you) or content marked "invisible"; server properties; custom XML data; and more. This type of information is often called *metadata*.

(Note that if you remove hidden data from a document, you might not be able to restore it.) To locate and remove this data, you can use the Office Document Inspector. The Document Inspector is available only in Word, Excel, and PowerPoint.

When the Document Inspector dialog box opens, you can control what type of content is inspected. Once the information is inspected, the dialog box displays any potential issues and allows you to remove the items. Be aware that the particulars of using Document Inspector vary slightly depending on whether you are using it in Word, Excel, or PowerPoint.

---

1 Click File.

2 Click Info.

3 Click Check for Issues.

4 Click Inspect Document.

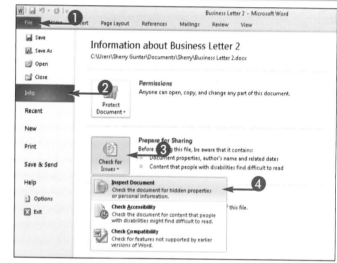

The Document Inspector dialog box opens.

5 Click what types of information you want inspected (☐ changes to ☑).

6 Click Inspect.

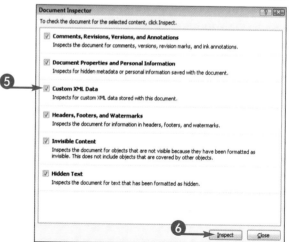

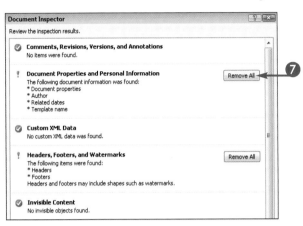

The document is inspected and any issues are listed.

7 Click Remove All to fix an issue.

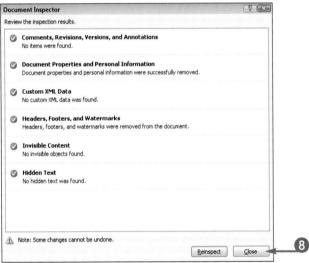

The Document Inspector removes the sensitive information.

8 Click Close.

Caution!

If you are not sure whether you want to remove the information flagged by Document Inspector, cancel the inspection and use the appropriate Office tools to view the information. For example, if document properties are flagged, view the document properties to see whether you want to eliminate them from the document. You cannot undo the effects of removing information with Document Inspector. You can, however, restore the removed information by closing the document without saving the changes that the inspection process made.

Important!

The Document Inspector does not remove metadata found in protected or restricted files, such as a document with a digital signature or restricted permissions. To get around this, be sure to run the Document Inspector before restricting or protecting the file.

If you are working on a document that contains sensitive information, you might want to encrypt it. That way, for someone to open the document and view its contents, he or she needs to enter a password, which you set. When you encrypt an Office document, you set a password for it; to open the document, the password is required.

Be aware that if you forget the password, you cannot open the document, even if you are the person who encrypted it. For this reason, it is imperative that you choose a password that you will not forget, or that you write the password down and keep it in a safe place. That said, the password should not be easy for others to guess. The strongest passwords contain at least eight characters and are composed of a mixture of uppercase and lowercase letters, numbers, and symbols. Avoid using common passwords such as pet names, birth dates, and so on.

① Click File.

② Click Info.

③ Click Protect Document, Protect Workbook, or Protect Presentation, depending on the program.

④ Click Encrypt with Password.

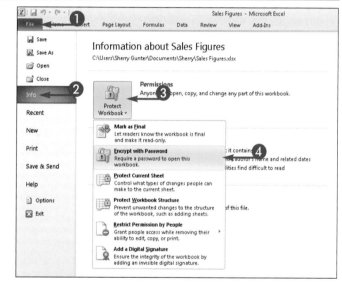

The Encrypt Document dialog box opens.

⑤ Type the password you want to use.

⑥ Click OK.

The Confirm Password dialog box opens.

⑦ Type the password again.

⑧ Click OK.

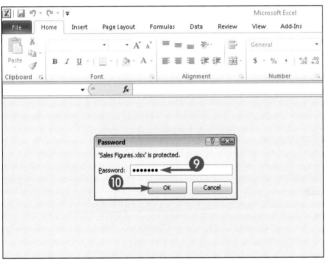

The next time you open the file, a prompt box appears for you to enter the new password.

⑨ Type the password.

⑩ Click OK.

Remove It!

To unencrypt a document, open it and revisit the Encrypt with Password feature. Click the File tab, click Info, and click a protection option (Protect Document, Protect Workbook, or Protect Presentation, depending on the program). Next, click Encrypt with Password. In the dialog box that opens, delete the password and click OK. This removes the password from the file.

Try This!

You can also assign a password to a file using the Save As dialog box. Click File, Save As to open the dialog box. After assigning a file name and storage location, click the Tools button and click General Options. Type a password in the Password to Open box and click OK. Retype the password again and click OK to assign it to the file. You can also use the General Options dialog box to restrict file sharing options for the document with a password to modify. Users cannot edit the document without knowing the password.

Add a Digital Signature

To authenticate an Office document, you can add a digital signature to it. First, however, you must create a digital ID and have a current digital certificate, which is a means of proving identity. A digital certificate is issued by a certificate authority, which is a trusted third-party entity. For a fee, you can get a digital signature from the Office Marketplace. (If you do not have a digital ID, you are prompted to create one as you complete this task.)

A digital signature contains a *message digest*, which contains a reduced version of the

document's contents, and a *private key*, which is used to encrypt the message digest on the signer's computer. When you sign a document, the encrypted version of the message digest is appended to the document; the digest is then decrypted by the recipient using the *public key*, included in the digital certificate associated with the signature. In this way, the recipient can confirm the origin of the document and that the contents of the document did not change during transit.

---

① Click File.

② Click Info.

③ Click Protect Document, Protect Workbook, or Protect Presentation, depending on the program.

④ Click Add a Digital Signature.

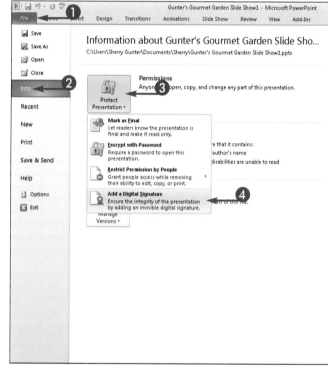

If you do not have a digital signature, this prompt box appears.

⑤ Click OK.

The Sign dialog box appears.

⑥ Type a note about the signature.

⑦ Click Sign.

A Signature Confirmation prompt box appears.

⑧ Click OK and the digital signature is added to the file and the file is marked as final.

● You can click View Signatures to review signatures assigned to the document.

Important!

You are not required to obtain a digital certificate from a certificate authority in order to create a digital ID and sign your Office documents; instead, you can create your own. To do so, click the Create Your Own Digital ID option instead of Get a Digital ID from a Microsoft Partner in the Get a Digital ID dialog box, which is shown automatically if no digital ID is present on your computer. Then, in the Create a Digital ID dialog box that appears, enter the requested information — name, e-mail address, organization, and location — and click Create. Note however, that when you share a file signed with a digital ID you created, it cannot be authenticated by users on other machines.

Recover an Unsaved Document

Office 2010 introduces a new feature to help you recover documents you did not save in Word, Excel, and PowerPoint. For example, perhaps you spent a great deal of time editing a Word document only to accidentally click Don't Save instead of Save when asked to save your changes. You can now recover your unsaved work with a few clicks.

By default, Word, Excel and PowerPoint are set up to automatically save versions of your file as you work on it, and keep a list of those autosaved files from your current session ready for recall. Autosaved drafts are stored in the DraftFiles folder. The autosaved versions are available only for a short time, however. Versions are kept for four days or until you reopen the file again.

If you close an editing session without saving, the Office program keeps the last auto saved version of the file and lists it in Backstage view among the Info settings. You can also find draft files listed in the Recent Documents list. A third way to locate drafts is through the Recover Unsaved Documents feature, which opens a dialog box where you can browse for files among the UnSavedFiles and DraftFiles folders.

1. Click File.
2. Click Info.
3. Click a recent draft listed here.

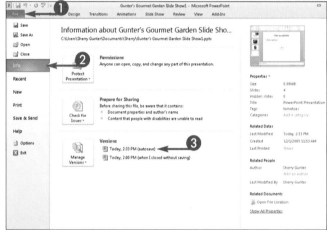

The recovered file opens.

4. Click Restore to restore the version.

A prompt box appears warning you that you are about to overwrite the previously saved version of the file.

⑤ Click OK.

● The draft is now the current version of the file.

Gunter's Gourmet Garden

Offering fresh produce for the discerning palate

Customize It!

By default, Word, Excel, and PowerPoint are set up to automatically save a file every 10 minutes. You can change this setting, if needed. To do so, click the File tab and click Options to open the program's Options dialog box. Click the Save tab to view the AutoRecover settings. You can change the amount of time for auto-saving, or you can turn off the feature entirely.

Remove It!

If you have been working on the same file for quite a while, you may have accumulated many drafts. You can delete them all if you no longer need them. Open the Backstage view and click the Info tab. Click the Manage Versions button and click Delete All Draft Versions. A prompt box appears asking if you are sure; click Yes or No.

Chapter 3

Boosting Your Productivity in Word

If you have a project that involves text of any kind — be it correspondence, a report, or what have you — you can harness the power of Word 2010 to quickly and easily generate a professional-looking document.

Word features a host of tools designed to improve your efficiency no matter what type of document you need to create, from prefabricated header and footer styles to building blocks for creating your own styles.

In addition to enabling you to generate your own documents, Word 2010 also eases the process of sharing your documents with others. For example, the program's Track Changes feature enables you to easily pinpoint where edits have been made and by whom. And of course, by providing features to expedite blogging, Word enables you to share your writing with the world.

Quick Steps

Word offers a gallery of several predefined header and footer designs, called *building blocks*, that you can apply. Headers appear in the top page margin area, and footers appear at the bottom. Headers and footers are a great way to place repeating information on your document pages, such as a document title, page numbers, company name, and so on. Word's predefined headers and footers make it easy to insert the information.

Alternatively, you can create your own header/footer building blocks — for example, one that contains your name and contact information in the color and font of your choice — and add that design to the gallery. That way, anytime you need to insert that particular header or footer, instead of reconstructing it, you can simply click it in the gallery.

In addition to creating header/footer building blocks, you can also create building blocks with other custom Office elements, such as cover pages, pull-quotes, and so on. Building blocks might also contain specific text or a graphic that you want to reuse throughout your Word documents.

Create a Header/ Footer Building Block

1. After designing the header or footer that you want to add to the header/footer gallery, select the text in the header/footer.

2. Click the Insert tab.

3. Click Header or Footer (depending on whether you created a header or footer).

4. Click Save Selection to Header Gallery or Save Selection to Footer Gallery.

   The Create New Building Block dialog box opens.

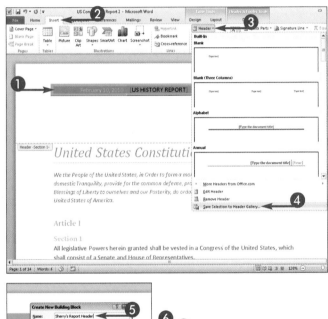

5. Type a name for the header or footer.

6. Specify the gallery in which the header or footer should reside.

7. Select a category for the header or footer.

   ● Optionally, you can type a description of the header or footer.

8. Click OK.

   The custom header/ footer is added to the gallery.

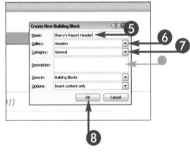

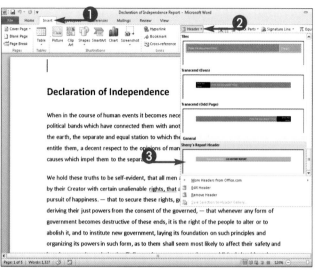

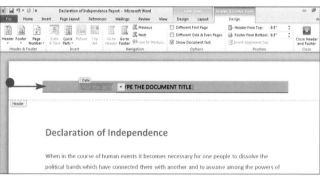

Apply a Header/Footer Building Block

1 With the document into which you want to insert the header or footer open, click the Insert tab.

2 Click Header or Footer.

3 Click the header or footer you want to add. (You might need to scroll down in the gallery to locate it.)

● The header or footer is inserted on the document page.

Customize It!

If your document contains section breaks, you can apply different headers and footers to each section. Click in the section for which you want to create a unique header or footer, click Header or Footer in the Insert tab, and click Edit Header or Edit Footer. The Design tab appears in the Ribbon; click Link to Previous to deselect it. Then create the new header/footer or insert a header/footer building block from the gallery. (Repeat for each section in your document.) Designing separate headers and footers for even and odd pages is similar; just click the Different Odd & Even Pages check box (☐ changes to ☑) in the Design tab instead of clicking Link to Previous and add the different headers/footers as normal.

Apply It!

You can easily add headers or footers in Word 2010 just by clicking the Insert tab on the Ribbon and clicking the Header or Footer buttons in the Header & Footer tool group. Either button displays a list of pre-set headers or footers to choose from; you can you create your own from scratch by clicking Edit Header or Edit Footer.

If you are new to the world of blogging, a *blog* is a sort of online journal. A blog might provide commentary on a topic as broad as food or politics, or as specific as the day-to-day activities of a single individual. Blogs can include text, images, links to other Web pages and blogs, and more.

Recent years have seen an explosion in the number of blogs on the Internet, with some estimates pegging the current number at more than 112,000,000. To accommodate this growing legion of bloggers, Microsoft has developed tools for composing and publishing

blogs to sites such as Windows Live Spaces and Blogger from within Word.

Composing blog posts within Word offers several advantages. First, you can use many of Word's formatting features, as well as its spelling- and grammar-checking capabilities on your blog entries. Second, you need not be connected to the Internet until you are ready to publish your piece.

To publish posts written in Word to your blog, you must first establish an account with a blogging site such as Blogger, and then register that account with Word.

① Click the File tab.

② Click New.

③ Double-click Blog post.

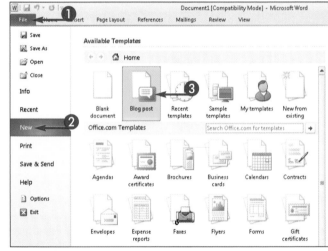

A Register a Blog Account prompt box appears if this is your first time creating a blog document.

④ Click Register Now to register your account with Word, or click Register Later if you want to complete the task after creating the blog. If you have already registered an account, skip to step 5.

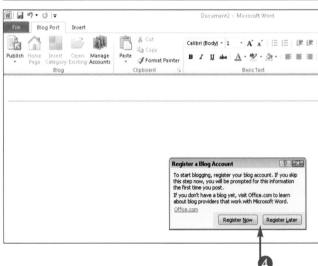

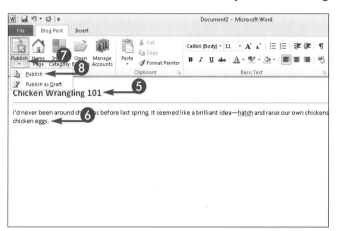

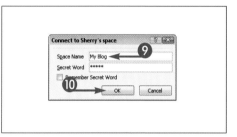

A blank blog post appears in the Word window.

⑤ Type a title for the post.

⑥ Type the text for your post, using Word's tools as needed to format and proofread the post.

⑦ Click Publish.

⑧ Click Publish or Publish as Draft.

A prompt box appears for you to log into your blog account.

⑨ Type in the appropriate logon information. Depending on your blog account, your logon information may vary.

⑩ Click OK to publish the blog.

Apply It!
If you are using Word to create a new blog post for the first time, Word prompts you to register your blog account. When it does, click Register an Account, click the Blog drop-down arrow, and choose your blog service provider. Click Next, enter the username and password for your blog account, click the Remember Password check box if you want Word to log you on automatically (☐ changes to ☑), and click OK.

Apply It!
Some blog providers automate the process of uploading photos to your blog; others require that you establish a separate account with a picture provider — that is, a site devoted solely to storing photos. To determine whether you need a picture provider account, check with your blog provider.

Navigating longer documents can be a bit daunting, especially when you are trying to locate a specific word or phrase. Word offers you several tools to help you search through a document. For simple word searches, the Navigation pane pops up and lets you search through a document, displaying any matches. You can use the pane's Search text box to enter the word or phrase you are looking for and immediately see any matches in the document.

The tried-and-true Find and Replace tool is the other go-to feature for searching through a document. You can use the Find portion of the tool to look for each occurrence of a word or phrase, and you can use the Replace portion of the tool to replace the word with different text. This makes quick work of finding a misspelled name and replacing it with the correct spelling, or searching a report for a particular price point and replacing it with a new price.

You can also use the Go To tab in the Find and Replace dialog box to jump to specific points in a document.

Finding Text

1 Click the Home tab.

2 Click the Find drop-down arrow.

3 Click Find.

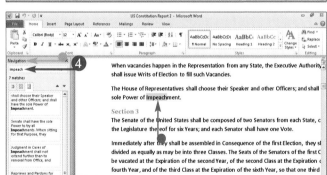

● The Navigation pane opens.

4 Type the word you want to look for in the Search text box.

● Word immediately highlights the first match in the document.

You can continue searching for more occurrences as needed.

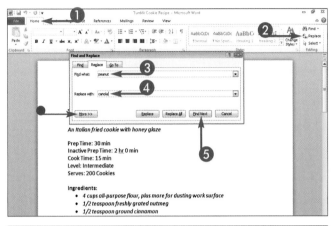

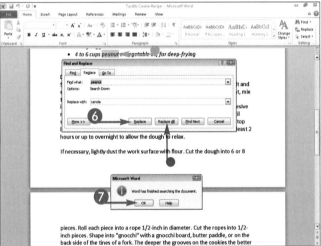

Finding and Replacing Text

① Click the Home tab.

② Click Replace.

The Find and Replace dialog box opens with the Replace tab displayed.

③ Type the word you want to look for in the Find What text box.

④ Type the replacement text in the Replace With text box.

● To view additional search criteria, click More and make your selections.

⑤ Click Find Next.

● Word highlights the first occurrence in the document.

⑥ Click Replace to replace the text.

● To replace all the occurrences, click Replace All.

⑦ When the search is complete, click OK.

More Options!

If you want to find a word and not replace it, just use the Find tab in the Find and Replace dialog box. It looks nearly identical to the Replace tab, only lacking the Replace With text box. To find a word, click the Home tab on the Ribbon and click Find to open the Navigation pane. You can type the word or phrase you are looking for in the Search box at the top of the pane; then press Enter to search for the first occurrence of the text.

Word's AutoCorrect feature has long been a tool for automatically correcting misspelled words in your documents. You can also use it to help automate some of your typing tasks. AutoCorrect comes loaded with a long list of commonly misspelled words, and because the feature is turned on automatically, you may have already noticed it kicking in when mistyping words. For example, if you type "teh," AutoCorrect automatically corrects the spelling to "the."

If you are like most people, you probably have a few words not in the AutoCorrect list that you consistently misspell. You can add them to AutoCorrect's repertoire and count on Word to correct the problems as they arise.

In addition to misspellings, you can turn a phrase into an AutoCorrect entry. For example, if your company name is particularly long, you can simply type an abbreviation and Word offers to fill in the rest for you, saving you the time and effort of activating the AutoText Gallery where you normally store snippets of preset text.

① Click the File tab.

② Click Options.

The Word Options dialog box opens.

③ Click Proofing.

④ Click AutoCorrect Options.

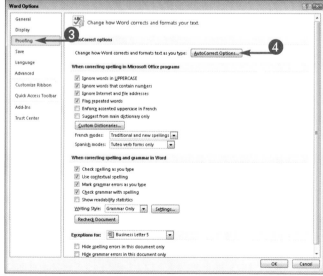

The AutoCorrect dialog box opens.

⑤ Click in the Replace box and type the misspelled word you want to add to the list.

⑥ Click in the With box and type the correct spelling of the word.

⑦ Click Add.

● AutoCorrect adds the word to the list.

⑧ Click OK.

⑨ Click OK to close the Word Options dialog box.

Did You Know?

To turn a long phrase into an AutoCorrect entry activated when you type the designated abbreviation, simply type the abbreviation in the Replace box in the AutoCorrect dialog box, and then type the full phrase in the With box. Click Add to add the entry to the listings.

Caution!

If you are having trouble adding a word in the With box in the AutoCorrect dialog box, click the Plain Text option (◎ changes to ◉) and then try again.

Emphasize Text with Drop Caps

Are you looking for a little drama to dress up your text? Word's drop caps feature might be just the thing you are looking for. You can use drop caps to quickly draw attention to the first letter in a paragraph. Commonly used in the printing business, a drop cap is the first letter in a paragraph that drops below the text line and extends into the second line of text, creating a large letter.

Throughout the history of printing, drop caps were used at the beginning of a chapter. You can use them in Word to the same effect.

You can use the Drop Cap dialog box to determine whether the letter drops within a paragraph or outside the paragraph margin. You can also change the drop cap's font, number of lines dropped, and even the distance between the drop cap and the rest of the paragraph text.

As with any formatting technique, it is good practice to use the drop cap feature sparingly. Too many on a page become quite distracting.

① Select the character you want to turn into a drop cap.

② Click the Insert tab on the Ribbon.

③ Click Drop Cap.

④ Click Drop Cap Options.

The Drop Cap dialog box opens.

⑤ Choose whether you want the position dropped or in the margin.

⑥ To choose a different font, click here and choose another.

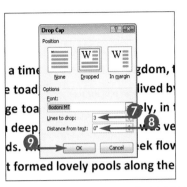

⑦ To change the number of lines dropped, type a new value here or use the spinner arrows to set a value.

⑧ To change the distance of the drop cap from the rest of the paragraph text, type a new value here or use the spinner arrows to set a value.

⑨ Click OK.

● Word applies the drop cap to the text.

O nce upon a time, in a faraway kingdom, there lived a little toad, named Todd. He lived by himself under a large toadstool, appropriately, in the middle of a deep, dark wood. Todd was very happy in the woods. There was a small creek flowing nearby that formed lovely pools along the way, and lots of fat, juicy bugs to eat. But one day, while hopping around the area, he ran into a stranger he had never seen in the woods before.

Try This!

For a quick drop cap without any changes to the settings, just click the Drop Cap button on the Insert tab and click Dropped or In Margin to immediately assign the effect to the selected letter in the document. You can also just click anywhere in a paragraph and apply a drop cap to the first letter using this technique.

Remove It!

To remove a drop cap, select it or click the paragraph containing the drop cap and click the Drop Cap button again, this time choosing None from the menu that appears. You can also open the Drop Cap dialog box and select None from the position options.

Set a New Default Line Spacing

As you are well aware, Word 2010 installs with a myriad of default settings in place for controlling everything from font and font size to margins as soon as you start the program. Although most of these settings work well for the average user, you may require different settings based on the type of work you do. Line spacing is an area in which individual document needs outweigh the defaults. By default, the line spacing is set to Multiple, which adds 1.15 points between each line of text. Happily, you can change the default line spacing to suit the way in which you work with Word. For example, if you produce a lot of

research and term papers, you may need to set the line spacing to Double, or if you are writing an article or book, you can change the setting to Single spacing.

Another spacing issue you may need to change is the default setting for paragraph spacing. By default, Word adds 10 points after a paragraph. This creates a gap of white space between paragraphs for you. Although this can be pleasing aesthetically, it does not work for all documents. You can change the spacing before and after paragraphs to suit your document needs.

① Click the Home tab on the Ribbon.

② Click the dialog box launcher in the Paragraph group on the Home tab.

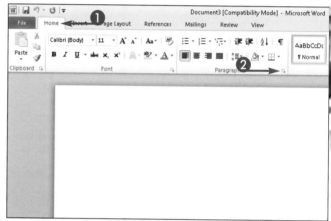

Word opens the Paragraph dialog box.

③ To set new line spacing, click the Line Spacing drop-down arrow.

④ Set a new line spacing to keep as your default setting.

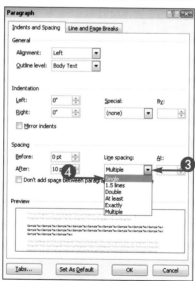

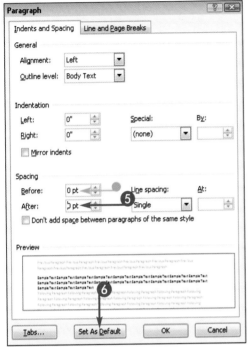

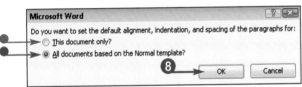

⑤ To set new paragraph spacing, click the After box and type a new value, or use the spinner arrows to change the value.

● Optionally, you can also set spacing to appear before each new paragraph, if needed.

⑥ Click the Set As Default button.

A prompt box appears asking how you want to save the changes.

⑦ Choose an option (⊙ changes to ⦿):

● Click This Document Only if you want to keep the new defaults in place only for the current document. New settings will not affect new documents you create.

● Click All Documents Based on the Normal Template to keep the new default settings for all new documents you create in Word.

⑧ Click OK to save the new settings.

Did You Know?
Document settings are saved along with the Normal template, the template that starts every new file you create using the New command or the new file that appears every time you open Word. This default template, though blank in appearance, has all the default settings in place for font, font size, and paragraph settings. To learn more about setting a default font and font size, see Chapter 1.

More Options!
You can also set other new defaults in the Paragraph dialog box for alignment, indentations, and line and page breaks. Simply open the dialog box and make the changes, then click the Set As Default button to make the changes permanent to the current document or all future documents based on the Normal template.

With some documents you create in Word, you may find yourself needing a horizontal line placed on the page. One way to add a line is to draw one using Word's Shapes. This option lets you draw the line precisely where you want it and to the length you want, even adding arrows or other flourishes to either end of the line. While offering you a variety of formatting options for the line, this method takes a little longer to perform.

If you are looking for a more straightforward line, consider using this little-known technique — you can type characters on your keyboard and turn them into an instant horizontal line on your document page. You can choose from a solid line that is a ½ point thick, a dotted line, a double line, a thick line, a wavy line, or even a thick decorative line.

This technique works only when you add the horizontal line to a new line of text in your document.

① Click where you want to insert the line in your document.

② Type three dashes (---).

③ Press Enter.

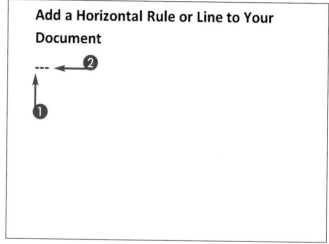

● Word inserts the line.

● To add a dashed line, type three asterisks (***) and press Enter.

● To add a double line, type three equal signs (===) and press Enter.

● To add a thick line, type three underscores (_ _ _) and press Enter.

● To add a wavy line, type three tildes (~~~) and press Enter.

● To add a thick, decorative line, type three pound signs (###) and press Enter.

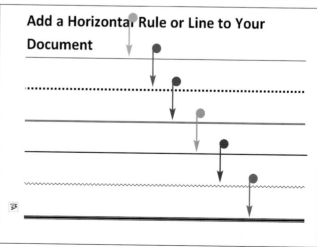

When you use numbered lists in your Word document, you may sometimes need to interrupt the numbered list with a paragraph, and then resume the list. Word's SmartTags can help you pick up where you left off with the numbering. For example, perhaps you are explaining a procedure step by step, but need to add a paragraph clarifying a feature or exception to the steps, and then restart the numbered list to continue on. Ordinarily, you might think you must start a new list to set a new number sequence. Save your time and use this technique instead.

When you reapply the numbers again after the interruption of a paragraph, Word first assumes you want to start a brand new numbered list and promptly adds the number 1 to the list as usual. A SmartTag icon also appears next to the number, resembling a lightning bolt icon. You can activate the SmartTag and choose the Continue Numbering option to resume the numbering sequence. If you choose to ignore the SmartTag, you can simply start a brand new numbered list instead if you just keep typing.

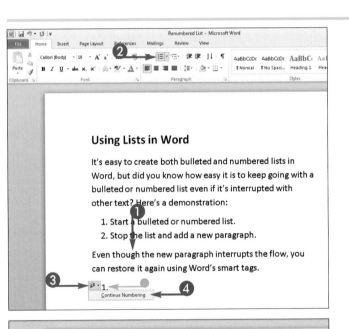

1 Type your list and paragraph.

2 Start the new numbered list on the next line by clicking the Numbering button on the Home tab.

● Word inserts the number 1 and displays a SmartTag icon.

3 Click the SmartTag.

4 Click Continue Numbering.

● Word changes the number to reflect where the previous list ended.

You can use partial or full borders to set off a paragraph within your document. For example, you can use a partial border to set off a pull-quote. A pull-quote is a sentence or two that you copy or extract from the document text to set off for visual and dramatic effect. Pull-quotes commonly appear in magazines and newspapers.

You can also set off an entire paragraph with a border, drawing attention to the text or message. For example, you can use a border to make the reader notice a paragraph of

important facts and statistics, or a paragraph of important instructions or details.

For additional border formatting, you can access the Borders and Shading dialog box. You can choose from a variety of line styles and thicknesses, and control the color of the line borders. You can also change border color, set partial borders, or even apply a 3-D, shadow, or custom style. You can preview your border selections in the dialog box before applying them to the actual paragraph.

Add a Border

1. Click inside of or select the paragraph to which you want to add a border.

2. Click the Home tab.

3. Click the Borders drop-down arrow.

4. Click the border you want to apply.

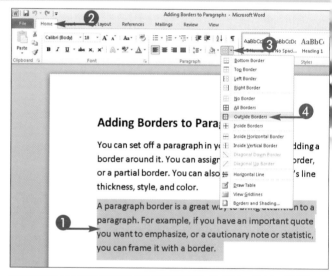

● Word applies the border.

● To apply background shading to the paragraph and border, click the Shading button and choose a color.

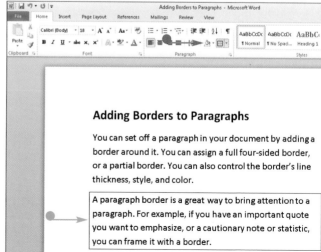

Format a Border

① Click inside of or select the paragraph containing the border you want to edit.

② Click the Borders drop-down arrow.

③ Click Borders and Shading.

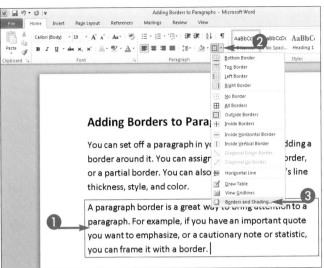

Adding Borders to Para[...]

You can set off a paragraph in yo[...] [...]dding a border around it. You can assign[...] [...]rder, or a partial border. You can also[...] [...]'s line thickness, style, and color.

A paragraph border is a great wa[...] [...]tion to a paragraph. For example, if you have an important quote you want to emphasize, or a cautionary note or statistic, you can frame it with a border.

The Borders and Shading dialog box opens.

④ Click the line style you want to apply.

⑤ Click here to change the line color.

⑥ Click here to set a new line thickness.

● The preview area lets you see what the formatting looks like before applying it.

● You can click these buttons to create partial borders around the paragraph.

⑦ Click OK.

● Word applies the changes to the border.

A paragraph border is a great way to bring attention to a paragraph. For example, if you have an important quote you want to emphasize, or a cautionary note or statistic, you can frame it with a border.

TIPS

Did You Know?

You can add a border to an entire page in your document. You can use the Borders and Shading dialog box to set a page border, line style, color, width, or even apply an artsy border complete with graphical elements. Simply click the Page Border tab in the Borders and Shading dialog box. You can also add page borders using the Page Borders button on the Ribbon's Page Layout tab. This route opens the same Borders and Shading dialog box to the Page Border tab.

Remove It!

To delete a paragraph border you no longer want, select the paragraph, click the Borders drop-down arrow on the Home tab, and then click No Border from the menu.

If you work in an environment in which you share your Word documents with others, you can use the program's Track Changes feature to help you keep track of changes made to the file by you and by others.

When Track Changes is enabled, Word tracks edits such as formatting changes and text additions and deletions you or other users make to the file. Additions appear inline in the text; deletions appear either inline in the text or in balloons in the right margin, depending on the document view. For example, in Word, using Draft view displays deletions inline and

comments appear only when you move the mouse pointer over the text; using Print Layout view, however, displays deletions inline and comments appear in balloons in the right margin. If multiple people review the document, each person's changes appear in a different color to help you keep track of who made what edits.

When you review a document that has been edited with Track Changes on, Word flags each change that each user makes in the document, which you can then accept or reject.

① To enable Word's Track Changes feature, click the Review tab in the Ribbon.

② Click Track Changes.

Note: If you click the Track Changes button drop-down arrow, you can access tracking options and change the username if you are not using your own computer to edit the file.

③ Edit the document, adding and deleting text and changing the formatting as needed.

④ To begin reviewing changes to an edited document, click at the beginning of the document.

Note: To turn off the Track Changes feature, click the Track Changes button a second time to disable it.

⑤ Click Next in the Review tab.

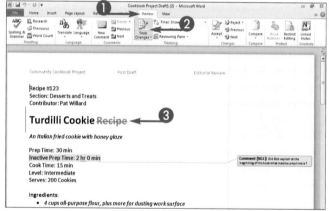

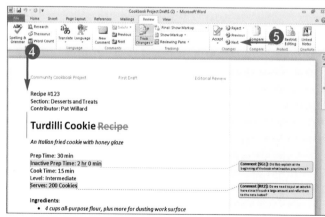

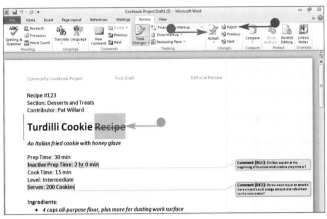

- Word highlights the first change in the document.

- To accept the change, click Accept in the Review tab.

- To reject the change, click Reject in the Review tab.

Note: To accept all changes in the document, click the drop-down arrow under Accept and click Accept All Changes in Document.

- Depending on which button you clicked, Word accepts (as shown here) or rejects the change.

- Word automatically highlights the next change in the document, which you can choose to accept or reject. You can continue accepting or rejecting changes as needed.

Did You Know?

By default, insertions appear as underlined text, and deletions appear either inline as strikethrough text, depending on the view. To change these and other settings, click the drop-down arrow beside Track Changes and choose Change Tracking Options. The Track Changes Options dialog box opens; change the settings as desired.

Try This!

You can click the Accept button's drop-down arrow and choose to accept all the changes in a document. You can also click the Reject button's drop-down arrow and choose to reject all the changes.

If you or someone else makes changes to a document without first enabling the Track Changes feature, but you want to determine exactly what edits were made, you can compare the edited document with the original.

When you compare an original document with an updated version, the result is a third file that flags the discrepancies between the two documents. (The two source documents — that is, the original and revised versions — remain unchanged.) These discrepancies look exactly like edits made with Track Changes enabled; that is, formatting changes and text additions and deletions become visible.

Additions and deletions appear inline in the text in Print Layout or Draft view. In Print Layout view, comments appear in balloons in the right margin. In Draft view, comments only appear when you move the mouse pointer over the text.

You review a file generated by comparing documents the same way you review a file that has been edited with Track Changes enabled. Word flags each change in the document, which you can then accept or reject.

① With the original version of the document open, click the Review tab.

② Click Compare.

③ Click Compare.

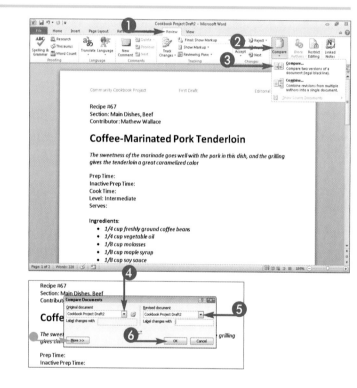

The Compare Documents dialog box appears.

④ Click here and choose the original version of the document you want to compare.

⑤ Click here and choose the revised version of the document.

Note: If the original or revised document does not appear in the list, click the Browse button (📁) to the right of the Original Document or Revised Document field and choose the desired document from the Open dialog box that appears.

● To view additional comparison features, click More.

⑥ Click OK.

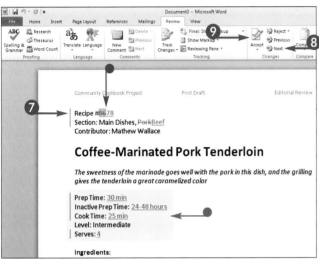

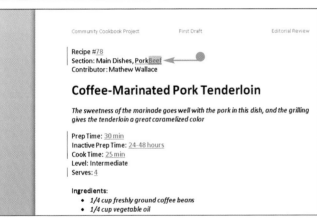

- Word compares the document by creating a new document file, flagging discrepancies such as text additions and deletions as well as formatting changes.

7 To begin reviewing the discrepancies, click at the beginning of the document.

8 Click Next on the Review tab.

- Word highlights the first discrepancy in the document.

9 Accept or reject the change. To accept the change, click Accept in the Review tab (as shown here). To reject the change, click Reject in the Review tab.

Note: To accept all changes in the document, click the down arrow under Accept and click Accept All Changes in Document.

- Depending on which button you clicked, Word accepts or rejects the change, and automatically highlights the next one in the document, which you can choose to accept or reject.

Did You Know?

To combine multiple revised files into a single document, click Compare on the Review tab and choose Combine. Select the original version of the document from the Original Document list, and select any of the reviewed versions from the Revised Document list. Click More and, under Show Changes In, click Original Document, and then click OK. Repeat for each revised version of the document.

More Options!

Another way to collaborate with others on a document is to use Word's Comments feature. To add a comment, select the text on which you want to comment, click New Comment in the Comments group of the Review tab, and type your comment in the balloon or field that appears.

Summarize Information with a Chart

Charts and graphs are a great way to illustrate your data. Word 2010 includes several tools you can use to add charts and graphs to your documents. For example, you can use the SmartArt feature to quickly insert preset diagrams and simply insert your own text elements to describe a process, hierarchy, or other procedure. If you need a tried-and-true data-based chart, you can tap into the power of Excel's chart-building tools to create pie charts, bar charts, surface charts, and more, all linked and alongside Word.

If you have Excel 2010 installed, you can take advantage of the program's advanced charting capabilities. When you activate the charting feature, Excel opens with a new worksheet ready for you to replace the placeholder text with your own chart data. Using columns, rows, and cells, you enter the raw data to make the chart. Over in Word, the same placeholder chart appears in your document in its full chart form. Data you add in Excel is immediately added to the Word chart, too.

When you create a chart, Word displays additional charting tabs on the Ribbon that you can use to format the chart.

If you do not have Excel installed, the Microsoft Graph feature opens instead.

① Click where you want to insert a chart and click the Insert tab.

② Click Chart.

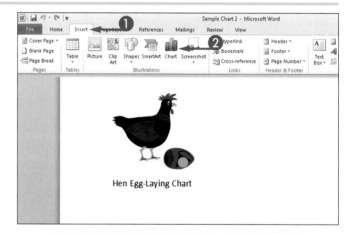

The Insert Chart dialog box opens.

③ Click the category of chart you want to make.

④ Click the chart type.

⑤ Click OK.

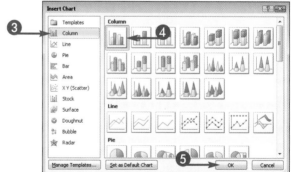

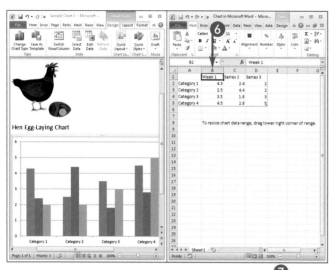

Excel opens and shares on-screen room with your Word document. A data sheet is ready to go in the worksheet, and a placeholder chart appears in the document.

6 Enter the data you want to chart using the worksheet cells.

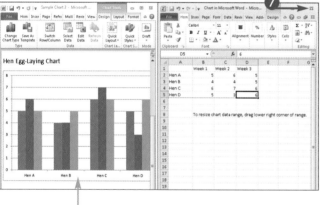

● The chart data is immediately updated in the Word document.

7 When finished entering your chart data, click Close to exit the Excel window.

Apply It!

To change your chart type, select the chart, click the Design tab under Chart Tools, and click the Change Chart Type button. This opens the Change Chart Type dialog box, which is exactly the same as the Insert Chart dialog box in step 3. Choose another chart type and click OK. The chart is immediately updated in the document. To delete a chart, select it in the document and press Delete.

More Options!

If you need to make changes to the chart data, you can reopen the datasheet in Excel and edit the cell data. Click the Design tab and click the Edit Data button. This reopens the Excel program window again with the chart data displayed. Simply edit the data and close Excel when you are finished. The chart is automatically updated in Word as you work.

4

Utilizing Word's Document Building Tools

Other Word tools help you save time by generating special elements for your documents. One such special element you can generate automatically in Word is a table of contents that contains all the headings in your document.

To ensure that your document meets the strict standards of academic and professional environments, you can use Word to insert footnotes and endnotes. Word numbers these footnotes, automatically updating them as you add, delete, and move text in your document. This saves you the time and trouble of tracking these items yourself.

Finally, to help you make your documents look more professional, Word includes tools for quickly inserting cross-references to other parts of your document.

Quick Steps

You can use Word to insert footnotes and endnotes in your document. A footnote is an explanatory note, usually in a smaller font, inserted at the bottom of a page to cite the source of or further explain information that appears on that page. The information to which the footnote pertains is flagged, usually with a superscript numeral, but sometimes with a symbol, such as a dagger symbol. Endnotes are like footnotes, but they appear at the end of a section or document rather than at the bottom of a page.

When you insert footnotes or endnotes in a document, Word automatically numbers them

for you. As you add, delete, and move text in your document, any associated footnotes or endnotes are likewise added, deleted, or moved, as well as renumbered. You can also easily convert footnotes into endnotes, or vice versa.

To delete a footnote or endnote, but leave the text in the document to which it refers intact, select the superscript numeral or symbol flagging the footnote or endnote and press Delete on your keyboard. Word deletes the flag as well as the note.

One more thing: You must be in Print Layout view to add a footnote or endnote.

---

1 Click in your document where you want to add the numeral or symbol indicating a footnote or endnote.

2 Click the References tab.

3 Click Insert Footnote or Insert Endnote.

- A superscript numeral or symbol appears at the cursor location. In this example, a footnote is added.

4 Type the information you want to include in the footnote or endnote.

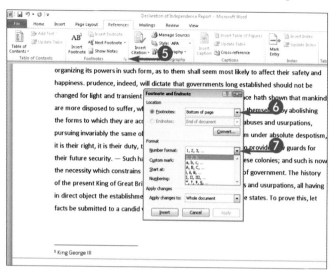

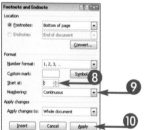

⑤ Click the dialog box launcher in the Footnotes group on the References tab.

The Footnote and Endnote dialog box appears.

⑥ Click here and select where on the page the footnote should appear.

⑦ Click here and select the desired number format.

⑧ Click here and select the number, letter, or symbol that should appear first.

⑨ Click here and specify whether the numbering should be continuous, restart at the beginning of each section, or restart at the beginning of each page.

⑩ Click Apply to apply your changes.

TIPS

Customize It!

If a footnote or endnote runs to a second page, you can add standard text, called a *continuation notice*, to it to indicate that it continues on the next page. To do so, first switch to Draft view, and then, in the References tab, click Show Notes in the Footnotes group. If prompted, specify whether you want to create a continuation notice for the footnotes or the endnotes in the document, click the Footnotes or Endnotes drop-down arrow and click Footnote Continuation Notice or Endnote Continuation Notice, and type the text you want to use in the notice.

Try This!

You can turn footnotes into endnotes, and endnotes into footnotes. To do this, click the Convert button located in the Footnote and Endnote dialog box. To open the dialog box, click the dialog box launcher (🔲) in the Footnotes group on the References tab. Next, click the Convert button to open the Convert Notes dialog box where you can choose a conversion option.

Generate a Table of Contents

If your document requires a table of contents (TOC), you can use Word to generate one automatically. By default, a TOC generated in Word contains text formatted in one of Word's predefined heading styles. Word generates the TOC by searching for these styles, copying text that has been formatted with them, and pasting it into the TOC. The TOC itself is simply a preformatted table, listing the headings and page numbers for each.

If you used custom styles in your document to create headings rather than Word's built-in styles, you can still generate a TOC; you simply indicate what styles Word should search for in your document when determining what the TOC should contain.

Regardless of whether you use Word's predefined heading styles to generate the TOC or you create a TOC that cites text formatted with custom styles, you can choose from Word's gallery of TOC styles to establish its look and feel.

Style Text as Headings

① Select text in your document that you want to style as a heading.

② Click the Home tab.

③ Click the More button.

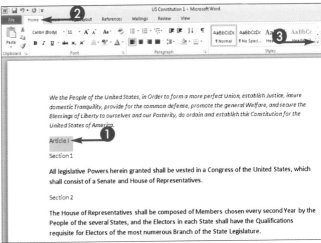

The Quick Style gallery appears.

④ Click the style you want to select.

● Word applies the style you chose to the selected text.

⑤ Repeat steps 3 and 4 to continue assigning styles throughout the document, as needed.

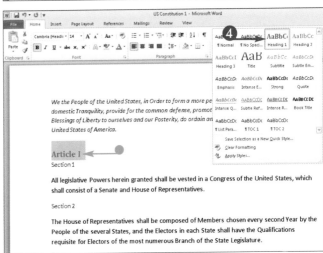

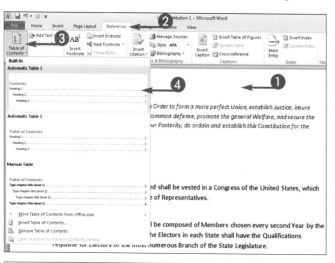

Generate a Table of Contents

1 Click the location in your document where you want to insert a TOC.

2 Click the References tab.

3 Click Table of Contents.

4 Choose the desired style.

Contents

● Word generates the TOC.

***Note:** To delete a TOC, click Table of Contents in the References tab's Table of Contents group and click Remove Table of Contents.*

TIPS

Customize It!

If you need to generate a TOC using custom styles rather than Word's predefined header styles, click Table of Contents on the References tab and choose Insert Table of Contents. The Table of Contents dialog box opens; click Options. In the Table of Contents Options dialog box, under Available Styles, locate the top-level heading style you applied to your document; then type **1** in the corresponding field to indicate that it should appear in the TOC as a level-1 heading. Repeat for additional heading styles, typing **2**, **3**, **4**, and so on to indicate their levels. Click OK to close the Table of Contents Options dialog box, and click OK again to close the Table of Contents dialog box.

Try This!

If you make changes to your document's headings, you can tell Word to update the table of contents. Just click the Update Table button on the Ribbon's References tab. This opens the Update Table of Contents dialog box where you can choose to update the entire table or just the page numbers.

Add a Cross-Reference

Suppose you want to insert text in one part of your document that refers the reader to a different part of the document for more information. To do so, you can insert a cross-reference. Cross-references can refer readers to text styled as a heading, to footnotes, to bookmarks, to captions, and to numbered paragraphs.

Before inserting a cross-reference, you will probably want to type some introductory text, such as "For more information, refer to." Then add the cross-reference after the text to complete the thought.

If the item to which a cross-reference refers is moved or changed, you can update the cross-reference to reflect the edit. To do so, select the cross-reference you want to update, right-click the selection, and click Update Field. To update all cross-references in the document, select the entire document rather than a single cross-reference.

Note that you can create cross-references only to items in the document that already exist. That is, you cannot create a cross-reference for a document element you have not yet created.

---

1 Type any text you want to precede the cross-reference — for example, *For more information, see page.*

2 Click the Insert tab.

3 Click Cross-reference.

The Cross-Reference dialog box opens.

4 Click here and select the type of document element to which the cross-reference will refer.

5 Click here and select what type of information the cross-reference will contain.

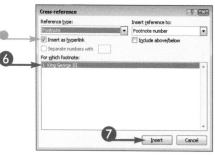

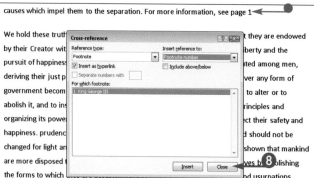

- Click Insert As Hyperlink
  (☐ changes to ☑) if
  you want readers to be
  able to jump directly to
  the item to which the
  cross-reference refers.

6 Select the specific item to
which the cross-reference
should refer.

7 Click Insert.

- Word inserts the
  cross-reference.

8 Click Close.

Note: *To remove a cross reference,
highlight it in the document and
press Delete. The reference is
immediately deleted.*

TIPS

More Options!
In order to cross-reference
figures or tables, you must
use Word's captioning
feature to create captions
for these elements first.

Did You Know?
Hyperlinks are another great way to cross-reference
users to other parts of your document. Hyperlinks
are links that, when clicked, jump the user to the
designated spot. To add a hyperlink, select the text,
click the Insert tab and click Hyperlink. This opens the
Insert Hyperlink dialog box where you can specify a
location to link to in the document based on heading
styles or bookmarks.

Optimizing Excel

You can use Excel to perform a wide variety of number-crunching tasks on data, from the simplest calculation to the most complex formula. You can also use Excel to track and manage large quantities of data such as inventories, price lists, and more. You can even use Excel as a database, entering and sorting records.

Data you enter into Excel is stored in a workbook. Each workbook contains individual worksheets, which hold your data. By default, Excel workbooks have three worksheets, each identified by a tab at the bottom of the screen, but you can add or remove worksheets as needed.

A worksheet is a grid, formed by columns and rows. Columns are labeled with letters, whereas rows are numbered. Every

intersection of a column and row creates a cell. Cells are the receptacles for your Excel data. Every cell in an Excel worksheet has a unique name, also called an address or cell reference, which consists of the column letter and row number, with the column listed first. For example, cell A1 is the first cell in the worksheet. The next cell to the right is B1.

A group of related cells in a worksheet is called a range. Excel identifies a range by the anchor points in the upper left and lower right corners of the range, separated by a colon. For example, the range A1:B3 includes cells A1, A2, A3, B1, B2, and B3. Ranges are particularly useful when you begin creating formulas that reference groups of cells.

Quick Steps

Automatically Open Your Favorite Workbook

By default, Excel opens a new, blank workbook every time you launch the program. This is fine and dandy if you want to start a new file each time you use Excel. But if you find yourself using the same spreadsheet every time you use Excel, you can tell the program to automatically open a particular workbook for you without being prompted.

To set up a workbook to open automatically, you can store the file in the XLSTART folder or create an alternate startup folder containing only the Excel file you want to launch. The XLSTART folder is created when you install

Excel on your computer, and the path to this folder varies depending on which operating system you are using. One way to find this folder path is to open the Trust Center to the Trusted Locations info. To make things easier, consider creating an alternate startup folder instead and save the workbook in the new folder. Once you have the required path and saved the file there, you can tell Excel to look for the workbook there every time you launch the program. You can also open more than one workbook at startup, if desired.

Create an Alternate Startup Folder

1. Open the workbook you want to launch at startup.

2. Click the File tab.

3. Click Save As.

   The Save As dialog box appears.

4. Navigate to the folder or drive where you want to add a new folder, if needed, and then click New Folder.

5. Excel adds a new folder; type a unique folder name and press Enter twice.

● Excel opens the new, empty folder.

6. Click Save to save the file to the new folder.

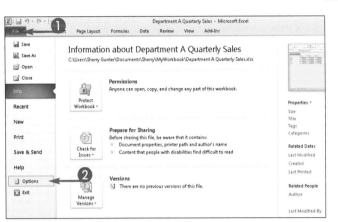

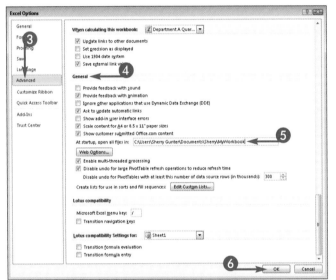

Designate a Startup File

1. Click the File tab.

2. Click Options.

The Excel Options dialog box appears.

3. Click Advanced.

4. Scroll down to the General settings.

5. In the At Startup, Open All Files In field, type the folder path to your alternate startup folder.

Note: Be sure to type in the full folder path accurately or Excel cannot locate your file.

6. Click OK.

The next time you open Excel, the designated file opens, too.

Note: To remove a startup file, repeat these steps and delete the path found in the Excel Options dialog box.

TIPS

More Options!

If you use Excel every day, you can tell your computer to open the program automatically when you turn on your computer. You can place a shortcut to the Excel program in your Windows XP, Windows Vista, or Windows 7 Startup folder. Look up your system's Startup folder and place a shortcut to Excel in the folder.

Caution!

If you ever run into trouble with automatically launching a workbook, such as a system crash, you may have to visit the Advanced resources and enable the workbook startup again. Click the File tab and click Options to open the Excel Options dialog box. Click Advanced, and check the folder path in the General settings. If you accidentally moved the file, you may need to fix the designated path listed.

Automate Data Entry with AutoFill

Often, the data that needs to be entered into an Excel worksheet is part of a series or pattern. In that case, you can use Excel's AutoFill feature to automate data entry.

For example, you might type the word **Monday** in your spreadsheet, and then use AutoFill to automatically enter the remaining days of the week. Alternatively, you might type **January**, and then use AutoFill to enter the remaining months of the year.

In addition to automating data entry using predefined data lists such as the ones described in the preceding paragraph, you can create your own custom data lists for use with Excel's AutoFill feature. For example, you might create a custom list that includes the names of co-workers who work on your team, or a list of products you regularly stock.

Along with enabling you to enter predefined or custom text series, AutoFill allows you to automatically populate cells with a numerical series or pattern.

AutoFill a Text Series

① Type the first entry in the text series.

② Click and drag the fill handle that appears in the lower right corner of the active cell across or down the number of cells that you want to fill.

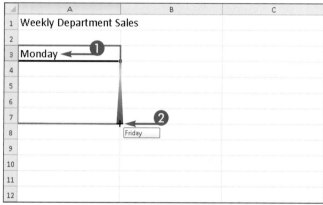

③ Release the mouse button and AutoFill fills in the text series.

● An Auto Fill Options button may appear, offering additional AutoFill options. For example, you can opt to copy the contents of the first cell into each cell rather than fill them with the series.

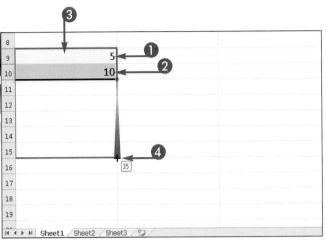

AutoFill a Number Series

① Type the first entry in the number series.

② In an adjacent cell, type the next entry in the number series.

③ Select both cells.

④ Click and drag the fill handle that appears in the lower right corner of the active cells across or down the number of cells you want to fill.

⑤ Release the mouse button and AutoFill fills in the number series.

● An Auto Fill Options button may appear, offering additional AutoFill options.

Customize It!

To add your own custom list to AutoFill's list library, first enter the contents of the list in your worksheet cells. Then do the following:

1. Select the cells containing the list you want to save.
2. Click the File tab.
3. Click Options to open the Excel Options dialog box.
4. Click Advanced.
5. Scroll down to the General group and click Edit Custom Lists.
6. In the Custom Lists dialog box, click Import. Excel adds the series to the custom lists. You can also create a new list by clicking Add and typing your list.
7. Click OK to close both dialog boxes.

A little-known organizing tip that most people never think about is formatting and naming the actual worksheet tabs. At the bottom of every worksheet, a tab marks the worksheet name and number in the stack. By default, the tabs are named Sheet1, Sheet2, and so on. The tabs themselves are very plain and nondescript. You can, however, use them to better organize your worksheet content.

For example you might color-code all the sheets related to the Sales Department in one color and all the sheets related to the Marketing Department in another. This can help you tell in a glance the purpose of each sheet in the workbook. You can assign different colors to different sheets using colors from Excel's color palette.

You can also rename sheets to better describe their content. A sheet named "Quarterly Sales" easily identifies what it contains and differentiates it from a worksheet named "Yearly Sales."

Color-Code Sheet Tabs

1 Right-click the tab you want to edit.

2 Click Tab Color.

3 Click a color from the color palette.

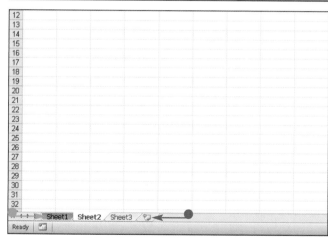

● Excel assigns the new color.

Note: Click another tab to see the color change in the tab you edited.

● Click Insert Worksheet to add new sheets, as needed.

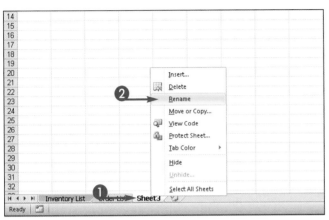

Name Sheet Tabs

① Right-click the tab you want to edit.

② Click Rename.

Note: *You can also double-click the tab name.*

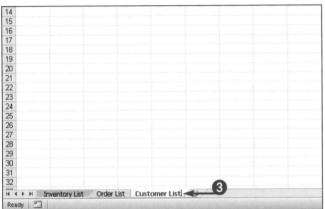

③ Type a new name.

④ Press Enter.

The name is assigned.

Remove It!

To remove color-coding from a worksheet tab, right-click it, click Tab Color on the pop-up menu, and then click No Color from the palette. This resets the tab to its original default status.

Try This!

If your workbook consists of dozens of sheets, you may tire of endlessly scrolling to find the one you want. Instead, try this trick: Right-click a scroll arrow to the left of the tab names. This displays a pop-up list of all the sheets in the workbook. Just click the one you want to view.

Protect Cells from Unauthorized Changes

Excel offers several ways to protect data, but the differences between them can be a bit confusing. For optimal protection, you can protect your entire workbook file with a password which allows only authorized users access. With this scenario, you can control who opens the file or who has permission to make edits.

You can also protect specific data within a spreadsheet. For example, if you share your workbook with a colleague, you may want to prevent changes in a cell or changes to workbook elements. You can choose to protect worksheet elements or protect the workbook structure, finding options for both on the Ribbon's Review tab.

Use the Protect Workbook feature to protect a workbook's structural elements, which include moving, deleting, hiding, or naming worksheets, adding new worksheets, or viewing hidden sheets. You can also use this feature to protect overall window structure, such as moving, resizing, or closing windows. Note that users can remove this level of workbook protection unless you assign a password.

You can use the Protect Sheet feature to prevent others from editing individual worksheet elements, such as cells, rows, columns, and formatting. Note that users can also turn off this protection feature unless you assign a password to the worksheet.

Protect Workbook Structure

1. Click the Review tab.

2. Click Protect Workbook.

   The Protect Structure and Windows dialog box opens.

3. Select which options you want to protect (□ changes to ☑).

4. To allow users to view the workbook but not make changes, type a password.

5. Click OK.

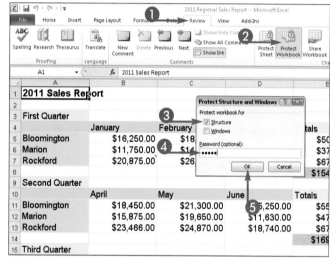

The Confirm Password dialog box appears.

6. Retype the password exactly as you typed it in step 4.

7. Click OK.

   Excel assigns the password to the workbook. The next time you or any other user opens the workbook, features for deleting, moving, and renaming worksheets will be unavailable.

Protect Worksheet Elements

1 Click the Review tab.

2 Click Protect Sheet.

   The Protect Sheet dialog box opens.

3 Make sure the Protect Worksheet and Contents of Locked Cells check box remains selected.

4 If you want users to be able to perform certain operations on the data in the worksheet, click the check box next to the desired operation (☐ changes to ☑).

5 To allow users to view the worksheet but not make changes, type a password.

6 Click OK.

   Excel prompts you to retype the password.

7 Retype the password exactly as you typed it in step 5.

8 Click OK.

   Excel assigns the password to the worksheet. The next time you or any other user opens the worksheet, only the features you selected will be available.

Caution!

The best passwords contain a mix of uppercase and lowercase letters, numbers, and symbols. Remembering your Excel passwords is critical. If you lose a password, you cannot make changes to a password-protected file. Consider writing the password down and keeping it in a safe place.

Remove It!

If you no longer want to password-protect a workbook or worksheet, you can easily remove the password protection. To unprotect a password-protected workbook, click the Review tab in the Ribbon and click Protect Workbook. The Unprotect Workbook dialog box appears; type the password and click OK. Unprotect a password-protected worksheet by right-clicking the sheet's tab and choosing Unprotect Sheet; in the Unprotect Sheet dialog box that opens, type the password and click OK.

Generate Random Numbers in Your Cells

You can use the RAND() function to generate random numbers in your worksheet cells. For example, you may want to generate random lottery numbers or fill your cells with random numbers for a template or as placeholder text. Depending on how you define the variables, you can generate a number between 0 and a maximum number that you specify. For example, if you define 100 as the maximum, the function randomly generates numbers between 0 and 100.

After assigning the function to one cell in your worksheet, you can use the fill handle to populate the other cells in the sheet with more

random numbers. The numbers you generate with the RAND() function take on the default numbering style for the cells. By default, Excel applies the General number format, with means that decimal numbers may appear.

To limit your random numbers to whole numbers, you can set the style to Number style and the decimal places to 0 using the Format Cells dialog box. You may want to do this before applying the function; from the Home tab, click the Number group's icon to open the Format Cells dialog box, select the Number category, and adjust the decimal places to suit your needs.

① Click inside the cell where you want to start the random numbering.

② Type **=RAND()*?**, replacing the *?* with the maximum random number you want Excel to generate.

③ Press Enter.

● Excel generates a random number in the cell.

④ Click and drag the selected cell's fill handle across or down as many cells as you want to fill with random numbers.

Excel fills the cells when you release the mouse button.

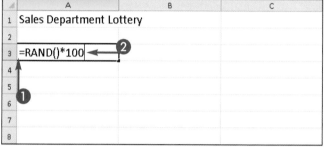

As you work with longer worksheets in Excel, it may become important to keep your column or row labels in view. The longer or wider your worksheet becomes, the more time you spend scrolling back to the top of the worksheet to see which heading is which. Excel has a freeze feature you can use to lock your row or column headings in place. You can freeze them into position so that they are always in view.

If you print out the worksheet, row and column headings appear as they normally do in their respective positions on the worksheet. You can, however, instruct Excel to print column or row headings on every printed page using the Page Setup dialog box. In the Page Setup group on the Page Layout tab, click the Page Setup icon to open the Page Setup dialog box. Click the Sheet tab, and under the Print titles section you can specify the row or column heading cell range to repeat.

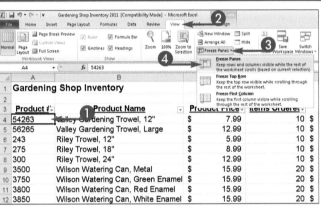

1. Click the cell below the row you want to freeze or to the right of the column you want to freeze.

2. Click the View tab.

3. Click Freeze Panes.

4. Click Freeze Panes.

● Excel adds a solid line in the worksheet to set off the frozen headings.

● When you scroll through the worksheet, the headings remain on-screen.

● To unfreeze the cells again, click Freeze Panes and choose Unfreeze Panes.

Insert a Comment in a Formula

You can add comments to your formulas to help explain the formula construction or purpose, or remind you to check something out about the formula. For example, you can add instructions about how to use the formula elsewhere in the worksheet.

Ordinarily, when you want to add a comment to your Excel worksheet, you use the comment text boxes. Comments can include anything from a note about a task to an explanation

about the data that a cell contains. To add a comment to a formula, you use the N() function instead of comment text boxes. The N() function enables you to add notes within the formula itself without affecting how the formula works.

The N() function is one of the many hundreds of functions available in Excel. To learn more about functions, check out the Excel Help feature.

① Click the cell containing the formula you want to edit.

② Click inside the Formula field where you want to insert a comment.

③ Type **+N("?")**, replacing the *?* with the comment text you want to add.

④ Press Enter.

● Excel adds the comment to the Formula field only, and the cell displays only the formula results.

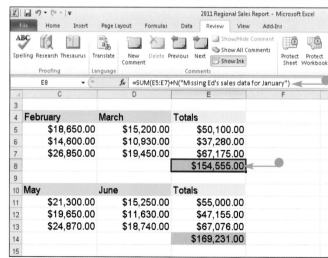

You can use the CONCATENATE function to join text from separate cells into a text string. For example, for a spreadsheet that lists the last, first, and middle names of a list of people in three separate columns, you can use the CONCATENATE function to join the names to print out or paste into another document.

When you use the CONCATENATE function, it is important to include spaces between the text strings to mimic spaces between names. In the formula, you can indicate spaces by entering actual spaces within quotes. If the

combined names require other punctuation, such as a comma, use a comma within the quotes between cell references. After establishing the formula for the first name in the list, copy the formula down the rows of the worksheet to join together the remaining names in the list.

You can use this same technique to join other types of text strings in Excel, such as product names and prices to print out for a customer, or dates and locations to give to a colleague.

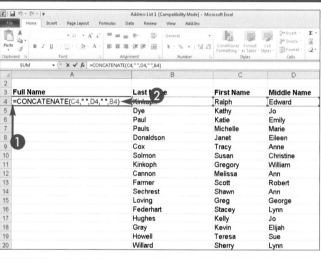

① Click inside the cell in which you want to display the text that you join together.

② Type **=CONCATENATE (?," ",?," ",?)**. Replace the *?* with cell references that contain the component names.

Note: Do not forget to press the spacebar between the quotation marks to add space between the names you join.

Note: Be sure to write the cell references in the order in which you want them to join together.

③ Press Enter.

● Excel combines the referenced cells into one cell.

Audit a Worksheet for Errors

If you see an error message, you should double-check your formula to ensure that you referenced the correct cells. One way to do so is to click the Smart Tag icon that Excel displays alongside any errors it detects; doing so opens a menu of options, including options for correcting the error. For example, you can click Help on This Error to find out more about the error message.

To help you with errors that arise when dealing with larger worksheets in Excel, you can use Excel's Formula Auditing tools to

examine and correct formula errors. In particular, the Error Checking feature looks through your worksheet for errors and helps you find solutions.

Auditing tools can trace the path of your formula components and check each cell reference that contributes to the formula. When tracing the relationships between cells, you can display tracer lines to find *precedents* (that is, cells referred to in a formula) and *dependents* (cells that contain formula results).

Check Errors

1. Click the Formulas tab.

2. Click Error Checking.

● Excel displays the Error Checking dialog box and highlights the first cell containing an error.

● To find help with an error, you can click here.

● To ignore the error, click Ignore Error.

● You can click Previous and Next to scroll through all of the errors on the worksheet.

3. To fix the error, click Edit in Formula Bar.

4. Make edits to the formula in the Formula bar.

In this example, a typo in the formula is corrected.

5. Click Resume.

When the error check is complete, a prompt box appears.

6. Click OK.

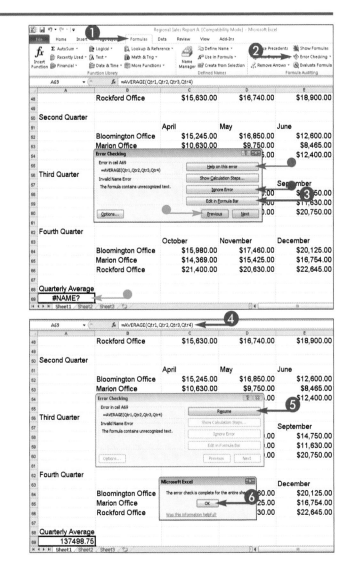

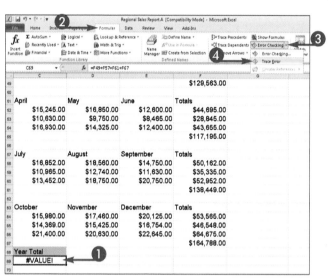

Trace Errors

① Click in the cell containing the formula, content, or error you want to trace.

② Click the Formulas tab.

③ Click the Error Checking drop-down arrow.

④ Click Trace Error.

- Excel displays trace lines from the current cell to any cells referenced in the formula.

- You can make changes to the cell contents or changes to the formula to correct the error.

⑤ Click Remove Arrows to turn off the trace lines.

TIPS

Did You Know?

You can click Evaluate Formula in the Formulas tab's Formula Auditing group to check over a formula or function step by step. Simply click the cell containing the formula you want to evaluate and click Evaluate Formula; Excel opens the Evaluate Formula dialog box, where you can evaluate each portion of the formula to check it for correct references and values.

Try This!

To quickly ascertain the relationships among various cells in your worksheet, click a cell, click the Formulas tab on the Ribbon, and click Trace Precedents or Trace Dependents in the Formula Auditing group. Excel displays trace lines from the current cell to related cells — that is, cells with formulas that reference it or vice versa.

You can use Excel to create projections in a manner similar to using the program's AutoFill feature. Excel offers a few options for creating projections. One is to determine a linear trend — that is, to add a step value (the difference between the first and next values in the series) to each subsequent value. Another is to assess a growth trend, in which the starting value is multiplied by the step value rather than added to the value in order to obtain the next value in the series, with the resulting product and

each subsequent product again being multiplied by the step value.

The easiest way to create a projection is to use Excel's automatic trending functionality. With it, you can simply right-click and drag to generate a projection. You can also create projections manually, entering a start value, a stop value, and the increment by which the trend should change. If your data is in chart form, you can still generate projections and even include a line in your chart to indicate the trend.

Determine a Linear Trend

1 Type the first known value.

2 In an adjacent cell, type the second known value.

3 Select both cells.

4 Position the mouse pointer over the fill handle that appears in the lower right corner of the active cells.

5 Right-click and drag across or down the number of cells you want to fill with linear trend data.

A context menu appears.

6 Click Linear Trend.

● Excel inserts the numbers that comprise the linear trend.

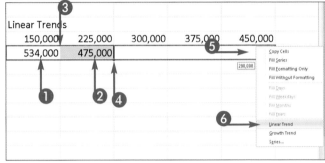

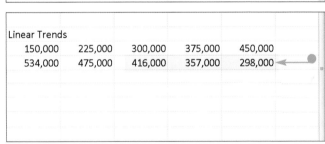

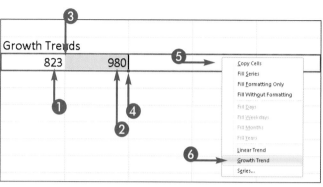

Determine a Growth Trend

1. Type the first known value.

2. In an adjacent cell, type the second known value.

3. Select both cells.

4. Position the mouse pointer over the fill handle that appears in the lower right corner of the active cells.

5. Right-click and drag across or down the number of cells you want to fill with growth trend data.

   A context menu appears.

6. Click Growth Trend.

   ● Excel inserts the numbers that comprise the growth trend.

TIPS

More Options!

Instead of automatically projecting linear and growth trends, you can project them manually. To do so, enter the first value in the series in a cell, and then select the cell. Next, click the Home tab and, in the Editing group, click Fill and select Series. Specify whether the series should cover columns or rows, enter the value by which the series should be increased, select Linear or Growth, select the value at which you want the series to stop, and click OK.

Did You Know?

You can use chart data to create projections, adding a trend line to your chart to represent the projection. For more information about creating charts in Excel and adding trend lines to those charts, see the Excel Help feature.

Create a Database Table

You can use an Excel worksheet to build a database table to manage large lists of data. A database table is simply a collection of related records, such as a phone directory, address list, inventory, and so on. After creating a database table, you can perform a variety of analysis, sorting, and filtering techniques on the data in the database table.

A database table is composed of fields, which break the table into manageable pieces. For example, a database table containing an address book will likely include fields with labels such

as Name, Address, and Phone Number. You fill in these fields to create a *database record*. A database record might consist of the name, address, and phone number of a single individual.

Before you create a database table in Excel, take a bit of time to plan it out, deciding what kind of data you want the database table to store and how it should be organized. Otherwise, you may later discover that you have omitted important fields and have to reorganize your database table.

---

① Add field labels to the top of the column table.

② Enter the first record in the row below the labels.

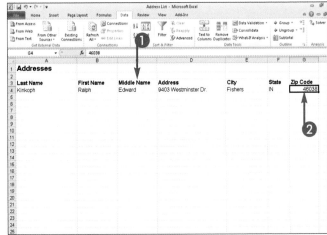

③ Continue adding records to build your table.

④ Select the data you want to convert into a database table.

⑤ Click the Insert tab.

⑥ Click Table.

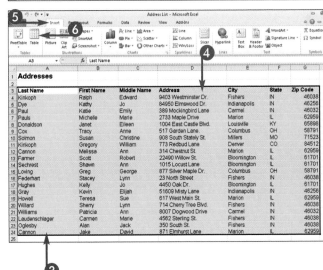

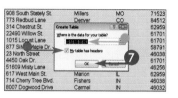

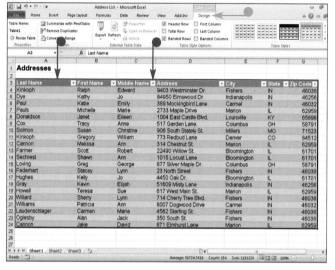

The Create Table dialog box opens.

● By default, the selected range appears here. If the range is not correct, you can select the correct cell references.

● Select this check box if it is necessary to include the headers in your table (☐ changes to ☑).

⑦ Click OK.

● Excel turns the data into a table, fills the cells of the table with table formatting, and displays filter drop-down arrows for each field.

● The Table Tools Design tab also appears on-screen.

● To filter a list, click here and select the data you want to filter out.

Did You Know?

Entering data into a table can be tedious. To speed up the task, you can use Excel's PickList feature, which is activated as soon as you create the first record in your database table and remembers the previous field entries so you can repeat them, if necessary:

1. Right-click a cell in a new record.
2. Click Pick From Drop-down List.

   A list of choices appears.
3. Click an entry to repeat it in the current cell.

Add and Edit Records Using Data Forms

If you have converted data in a spreadsheet into a database table, you can add information to that table using a data form instead of typing it directly into the cells in the worksheet. (For help converting data in Excel spreadsheets into database tables, refer to the preceding task.)

In Excel, data forms are special dialog boxes that contain all the fields in your table. For example, if your database table contains a Name field, an Address field, a City field, a State field, and a ZIP field, so too will the database table's data form dialog box. You can type the information for a database record into the dialog box rather than into the spreadsheet. (Note that you can also edit existing records from a data form dialog box.)

To access the command used to display the data form dialog box, you must first add it to the Quick Access toolbar. To do so, click the Customize Quick Access Toolbar button at the end of the toolbar, click More Commands, and, in the dialog box that appears, click the Choose Commands From drop-down arrow and choose Commands Not in the Ribbon. Then scroll down the list and click Form, click the Add button, and click OK.

---

① Click the first cell of any record in your database table.

② Click the Form button.

A data form dialog box opens displaying data from the record you selected in step 1.

③ Click New.

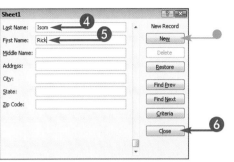

④ Type the data for the first field in the new record and press Tab.

⑤ Repeat step 4 to continue filling out the fields.

● To fill out another new record, click New.

⑥ When finished entering records, click Close.

● Excel adds the new record(s) to the database table.

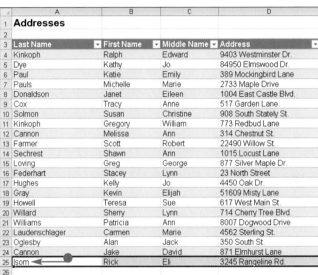

TIPS

Try This!

Click the Find Prev and Find Next buttons in the data form dialog box to navigate records in a database table. Edit records by typing over the existing values in the data form dialog box's fields.

Delete It!

To delete a record, click the first cell in any record in the table and open the data form dialog box. Then click the Find Prev or Find Next button as many times as necessary to locate the record you want to delete. Finally, click the Delete button in the dialog box, and click OK to confirm the deletion. Alternatively, select the row in the table that contains the record you want to delete and then press Delete. This deletes the row content. To remove the row entirely, right-click the row number and click Delete.

Polishing Your Spreadsheet Data

Being able to crunch numbers or build database tables is of little use if your worksheet data is difficult or impossible for others to comprehend. Fortunately, you can mitigate this by liberally applying some of Excel's formatting tools. For example, you can apply themes to your workbooks to create a more polished and professional look, as well as add colors, patterns, and borders to cells to make them stand out. You can even use digital images as backgrounds in your worksheets.

To draw attention to cells that meet criteria you set, you can apply conditional formatting. For example, you might set a rule to highlight cells that contain values greater than, less than, equal to, or between a range of specified values. This enables you to detect problems, patterns, and trends at a glance.

Another way to display your data is in chart form. Whether you are depicting rising or falling sales or actual costs compared to projected costs, charts can make it easy for others to understand your data.

To ensure that others can read the data in your worksheet's cells, you can fine-tune its appearance by adding gridlines, enabling Excel's text-wrapping feature (which automatically increases a cell's row height to make room for the data it contains), and changing text orientation within the cells. This chapter introduces you to a variety of tasks designed to help you make your data look great and print great so you can convey your information with ease and clarity.

Quick Steps

Tired of applying formatting to your worksheet data? You can use Excel's Themes Gallery to apply a combination of preset formatting settings to your spreadsheet to create an instant, professional looking spreadsheet.

To use themes to their fullest, you must apply styles to your worksheet, such as a heading style to any column headings or a title style to the worksheet title. Applying styles is easy, just select the cell to which you want to apply the style, click the Home tab, click the Cell Styles button in the Styles group, and choose a style.

If you want the worksheet to display the theme's background color, you must apply a background color beforehand. Select the cells to which the color should be applied, click the Home tab, click the drop-down arrow next to the Fill Color button, and choose a color.

You can modify a theme you have applied using the Colors, Fonts, and Effects buttons in the Page Layout tab's Themes group and then save the modified theme for reuse.

Apply a Theme

1 Click the Page Layout tab.

2 Click Themes.

● Excel displays the Themes Gallery.

3 Click the theme you want to apply.

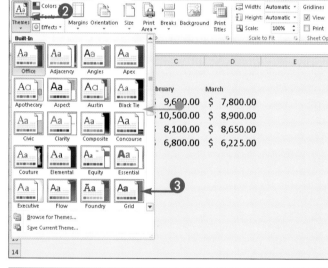

● Excel applies the theme to the worksheet.

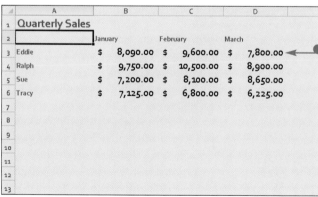

Save a Theme

1 Modify the theme you want to save.

In this example, the font, size, and color are modified.

2 Click the Page Layout tab.

3 Click Themes.

4 Click Save Current Theme.

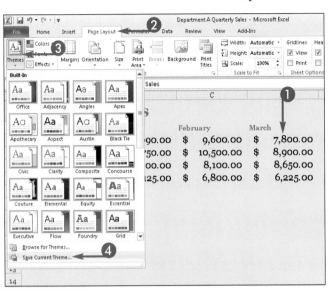

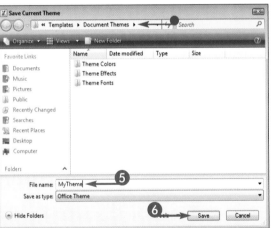

The Save Current Theme dialog box opens.

● Themes are stored in a default location among the other Office themes and templates.

5 Type a unique name for the theme.

6 Click Save to save the theme.

Did You Know?

You can find more themes to use with your Office 2010 programs online. Themes are just templates with ready-made formatting for the design appearance of a spreadsheet or other Office document. Although the Themes Gallery in Excel displays a wide variety of themes, you may be looking for something more stylized. Check out the Microsoft Office Web site (http://office2010.microsoft.com) and browse for more themes you can download and use.

Remove It!

If you create a custom theme and decide you no longer want it in your library, you can easily remove it. Display the Themes Gallery on the Page Layout tab and right-click the custom theme name. Next, click the Delete command. This opens the Microsoft Excel prompt box asking if you want to delete the theme. Click Yes and the theme is removed.

Gridlines are an essential element of every Excel worksheet you display. Gridlines are key to helping you maintain order and keeping your data-entry tasks organized and easy to perform. Gridlines help you keep your contents lined up properly in their respective cells.

By default, the gridlines appear as faint bluish-gray lines that define column and row borders and the cells contained within. Depending on how busy your worksheet becomes as you enter more and more data, it is not always easy

to see the gridlines. Thankfully, you can customize the worksheet and substitute another color setting for gridlines.

You can change the gridline color by accessing the Excel Options dialog box and the Advanced options. If, after assigning a new color, you prefer to return to the default setting, simply revisit the dialog box settings and switch back to Automatic as your color choice for the gridlines.

① Click the File tab.

② Click Options.

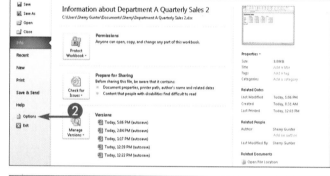

The Excel Options dialog box appears.

③ Click Advanced.

④ Scroll down to the Display Options for This Worksheet section.

⑤ Click the Gridline Color button.

⑥ Click a new color.

⑦ Click OK.

● The color is assigned to the current worksheet.

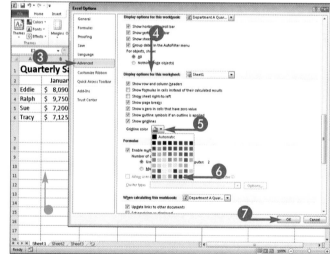

Gridlines make it easier to read a worksheet. By default, gridlines appear on-screen, but not in printed versions of your worksheet. If you plan to print your worksheet, you might want to set up Excel to print it with the gridlines displayed. Doing so makes the printed worksheet a bit easier to read — although be aware that printing with gridlines takes a bit longer than printing without them.

You can apply two methods to activate gridline printing. You can click the Print check box (☐ changes to ☑) on the Page Layout tab under the Gridlines settings, or you can use Excel's Page Setup dialog box to activate gridline printing. In addition to specifying that gridlines be printed, you can also choose other print-related options in Excel in the Page Setup dialog box.

When you are finally ready to print the worksheet, you can use the Print settings available in Backstage view; click the File tab and click Print to display all the printing options and the command for printing the workbook. You can also see a preview of what your printed gridlines will look like.

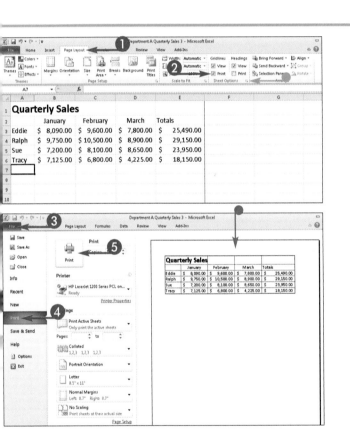

① Click the Page Layout tab.

② In the Sheet Options group under Gridlines, click Print (☐ changes to ☑).

● If you want Excel to print gridlines and you want to alter other print settings, click the Sheet Options icon to display the Page Setup dialog box.

③ Click the File tab.

④ Click Print.

● You can preview the printed gridlines and cells here.

⑤ Click Print to print out the worksheet.

Add a Background Color, Pattern, or Image

You can add a background color or pattern to the cells in your worksheet to make it more visually appealing. Excel offers a variety of preset colors and patterns from which you can choose to create just the right look for your worksheet data.

The easiest way to apply a quick background color or shading to selected cells is to apply a fill color. Just click the Fill Color button on the Home tab. For more fill options, including patterns, you can open the Format Cells dialog box to customize the fill. Anytime you choose

a background color you need to be careful not to choose a color that makes it difficult to read the cell data.

In addition to adding a color or pattern to cells to serve as a background for your worksheet, you can also add a photo or other digital image. For example, if your worksheet documents sales, you might add a picture of a product. As with fill color, you need to choose an image that does not clash with the cell data or render it illegible. If it does conflict, you might need to change the color of the worksheet data.

Add a Fill Pattern

① Select the cells to which you want to apply a background color or pattern.

② Click the Home tab.

③ Click the Font group's dialog box launcher.

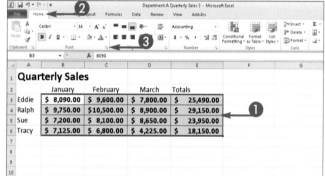

The Format Cells dialog box opens.

④ Click the Fill tab.

● To apply a background color, click the desired color in the palette.

● To assign a gradient fill effect, click Fill Effects and customize the settings.

⑤ Click here and then select the desired pattern color.

⑥ Click here and then select a pattern.

⑦ Click OK.

● Excel applies the selected background pattern.

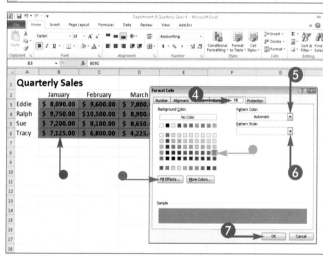

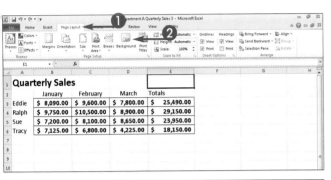

Add a Background Image

1 Click the Page Layout tab.

2 Click Background.

The Sheet Background dialog box opens.

3 Locate and click the image you want to apply to the background.

4 Click Insert.

● Excel applies the selected background image.

TIPS

Try This!

Even if you do not have a color printer, you can take advantage of the various shades of gray to add background colors to your worksheet cells. You can also experiment with the palette of solid colors to create varying degrees of background shading in grayscale tones.

Remove It!

To remove all of the formatting in a cell, including background colors or patterns, select the cell, click the Home tab, and then click Cell Styles. In the gallery of styles that appears, click Normal. This removes all the formatting that has been applied. To delete a background image, click Delete Background in the Page Layout tab.

Color-Code Your Data with Conditional Formatting

You can use Excel's conditional formatting functionality to assign certain formatting only when the value of the cell meets a specified condition. This enables you to detect problems, patterns, and trends at a glance.

Excel offers several predefined rules for conditional formatting. For example, you can set a rule to highlight cells that contain values greater than, less than, equal to, or between a range of specified values; specific text or dates; duplicate values; the top ten or bottom ten values; above-average or below-average values; and more.

You can format cells that meet conditions you set by changing the font or cell background. You can also apply data bars, where the length of the bar represents the value in the cell; color scales, which enable you to compare cells in a range using a gradation of color; and icon sets, which enable you to classify data into categories with each category represented by a particular icon.

If none of the predefined rules suits your needs, you can modify or create a new one.

---

1 Select the cell or range to which you want to apply conditional formatting.

2 Click the Home tab.

3 Click Conditional Formatting.

4 Click the desired rule category (here, Highlight Cells Rules).

5 Click the desired rule (here, Less Than).

A dialog box appears, enabling you to specify the desired conditions.

Note: *Depending on the rule you selected, the dialog box settings will vary.*

6 Enter the values or text for the condition. In this example, the cell is formatted if its value is less than 20,000.

7 Click here and select a format to apply.

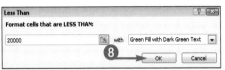

8 Click OK.

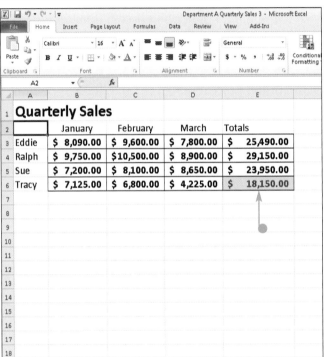

● Excel applies the conditional formatting to any cells that meet the established conditions. In this example, the value is less than 20,000.

Try This!

To quickly locate cells to which a conditional formatting rule has been applied, click any cell in the sheet, click the Home tab, click Find & Select, and click Conditional Formatting. To find only those cells with the same conditional formatting, click a cell to which said formatting has been applied, click Find & Select, choose Go To Special, click Conditional Formats, and click Same under Data Validation.

Remove It!

To remove conditional formatting from a worksheet, click the Home tab, click Conditional Formatting, point to Clear Rules, and then click Clear Rules from Entire Sheet. To remove conditional formatting from certain cells only, select the cells, click the Home tab, click Conditional Formatting, point to Clear Rules, and then click Clear Rules from Selected Cells.

You may run into situations where the text you need to enter is wider than the cell meant to hold it, especially if your worksheet contains cells with lengthy text. By default, when the amount of data in a cell exceeds the cell's width, the data remains on one line. If the cells to the right of the cell in question are empty, this poses no problem because the data simply stretches across subsequent cells.

If, however, the cells to the right contain data, those cells will obscure any text that spans beyond the cell in question. To view the data in its entirety, you must click the cell that contains the data and look at the Formula bar.

If you want to be able to see the data in its entirety within the cell, you can turn on Excel's Wrap Text feature. When you do, data in the cell wraps to the next line, with the height of the row containing the cell increasing to make room.

① Click to select the cell or cells that you want to edit.

② Click the Home tab.

③ Click the Wrap Text button.

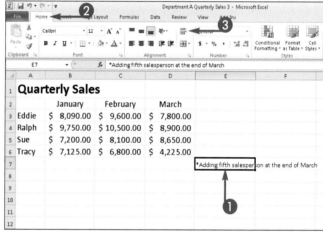

● Excel applies text-wrapping to the selected cell(s).

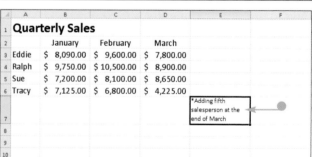

You can add visual interest to your worksheet text by changing the text orientation, such as angling the text upwards or downwards in the cell. You might use this technique to make a long column heading take up less horizontal space on the worksheet. This can often prevent Excel from spreading the data to a second document page for printing. Angling the column headings is also a great way to make the text visually appealing.

Using the Orientation tool, you can rotate text to a diagonal angle or orient the text straight up or down in a cell. For a quick orientation assignment, simply click the Orientation button and choose the desired setting. For more control over the effect, open the Format Cells dialog box and set an exact degree of rotation, as shown in this task.

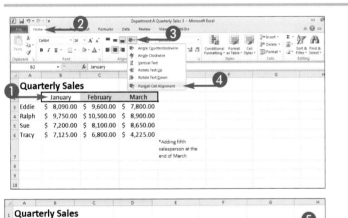

1 Select the cell or range you want to edit.

2 Click the Home tab.

3 Click the Orientation button.

4 Click Format Cell Alignment.

The Format Cells dialog box opens to the Alignment tab.

5 Click an orientation setting.

● You can also enter an exact value in the Degrees box or click the spinner arrows to set a value.

6 Click OK.

● Excel applies the new orientation.

By default, Excel aligns all printed data to the left and top margins of the page when you print it out, unless you specify otherwise. You may find that some of your worksheets look better if you center the data on the printed page. You can use the Page Setup dialog box to determine how you want the printed data to align on the page.

You can select the Horizontally option to center data between the left and right margins,

or the Vertically option to center the data between the top and bottom margins. You can also apply both centering alignments to the same page at the same time.

In addition, you can also use the Page Setup dialog box to control other margin aspects for the printed page, such as setting exact margin values or margins for header or footer text.

① Click the Page Layout tab.

② Click the Page Setup group's dialog box launcher.

The Page Setup dialog box appears.

③ Click the Margins tab.

④ Click a centering option (☐ changes to ☑).

⑤ Click OK.

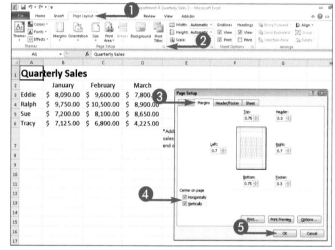

● The new setting is applied when you print the worksheet. In this example, the data is centered both horizontally and vertically.

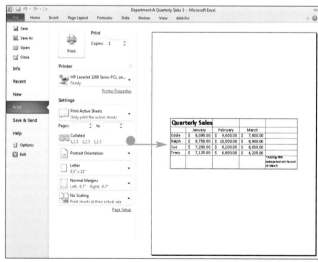

Another way to make your worksheets more visually appealing is by centering title text, such as a range heading, across several columns. Ordinarily, when you want to center text across several worksheet cells, you must use the Merge Cells command. This command creates one large cell to contain the title text. However, if you need to cut or copy the rows or columns that intersect with the merged cell, Excel does not allow you to do so. You may

also find it difficult to perform a sort on a list that contains a merged cell.

Fortunately, there is another technique that centers your title text without combining worksheet cells. Using the Center Across Selection option in the Format Cells dialog box, you can achieve the same appearance as if you merged the cells. This technique leaves intersecting rows and columns safe for cutting and copying later.

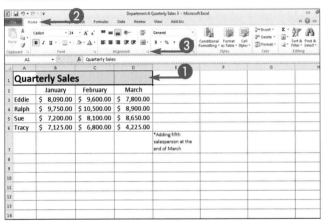

1 Click the cell containing the text you want to center and the cells you want to span.

2 Click the Home tab.

3 Click the Alignment group's dialog box launcher.

The Format Cells dialog box opens to the Alignment tab.

4 Click the Horizontal drop-down arrow.

5 Click Center Across Selection.

6 Click OK.

● Excel centers the text.

Increasing PowerPoint's Potential

You can use PowerPoint to create presentations to convey all kinds of messages to an audience. For example, you might employ PowerPoint to present an idea to a prospective client, explain a concept or procedure to employees, or teach a class about a new subject. Your presentation can include words, graphics, media clips, charts, tables, and more.

When creating a presentation, you build an outline, with each first-level heading in the outline serving as the title of an individual slide. Second-level headings appear as bullet points; third-level headings appear as sub-bullets; and so on.

Once your presentation is set up, you can set a time length for the display of each slide. If, for example, you want the presentation to play back in a booth at a trade show, you can set it up to run automatically, such that it requires no external input or management. If, on the other hand, you are the presenter, you can print out speaker notes for your use during the show. To help your audience better follow along, you can also print handouts, which contain the slides in your presentation.

You can place your presentation on the Web, enabling you to widen your audience substantially.

Convert a Word Document into a Presentation

Perhaps you have invested significant time generating a document in Word, and your boss asks you to give a presentation about that document. Instead of retyping the information from the document and reproducing it all over again in PowerPoint, you can import it. This can really save you time and effort.

When you import a Word document into PowerPoint, PowerPoint translates any text in the Word document that is represented in Word's Outline view into a PowerPoint outline. Any heading in the document styled with Word's Heading 1 style appears as a slide title atop a new slide. Second-level headings become bullet points, third-level headings become second-level bullet points, and so on. Normal-style text between the headings is omitted.

You can edit a presentation generated from a Word document just as you would any other presentation: by selecting the slide you want to edit and making the necessary changes.

① Click the File tab.

② Click Open.

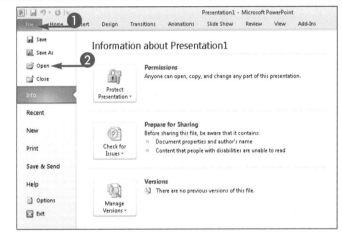

The Open dialog box appears.

③ Click the file types drop-down arrow.

④ Click All Outlines.

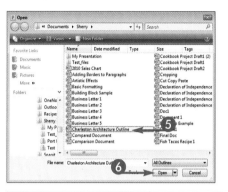

⑤ Navigate to and select the Word file you want to use.

⑥ Click Open.

● PowerPoint imports the Word document, adding all first-level headings as slide titles, second-level headings as bullets, and so on.

Caution!
Before importing a Word document, make sure the appropriate headings are applied. You can use Word's Outlining feature to create easy outlines using heading styles, such as Heading 1, Heading 2, Body text, and so on. To switch to Outline view, click the View tab on the Ribbon and click Outline. This opens the Outlining tab where you can use the tools to create an outline for a presentation.

Organize a Presentation into Sections

Giant presentations can be cumbersome and difficult to navigate when creating content and organizing slides. Thankfully, PowerPoint 2010 offers a new tool to make handling larger presentations easier by assigning sections. You can easily keep track of a group of slides that share the same section, or hand off a section to a colleague for collaboration. You can even use sections to help you systematize topics for a brand-new presentation.

Sections are labeled as such in the Slides pane of Normal view as well as in Slide Sorter view.

When you add a new section, PowerPoint assigns a default section name which you can then replace with something more meaningful.

You can expand and collapse the sections in the Slides pane in Normal view to help you view just the slides you want to work with, and you can move sections up and down in the slide order. To organize your slides, simply move them from one section or another by dragging them in the Slides pane or Slide Sorter view. You can also remove sections you no longer need.

① Click where you want to insert a section in the Slides pane.

② Click the Home tab.

③ Click Section.

④ Click Add Section.

● PowerPoint inserts a new section.

⑤ Right-click the section name.

⑥ Click Rename Section.

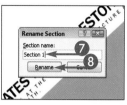

The Rename Section dialog box opens.

⑦ Type a name for the section.

⑧ Click Rename.

● PowerPoint renames the section.

● You can add more sections to your presentation as needed.

TIPS

Try This!

To move a section to another spot in the presentation, right-click its name and chose Move Section Up or Move Section Down. You can also drag and drop section names in Slide Sorter view to move sections. Simply click and drag the section title to a new location in the presentation. All the accompanying slides move with the section head.

Remove It!

PowerPoint offers you several ways to handle removing a section in a presentation. To remove a section only, but leave the slides intact where they are, right-click the section name and choose Remove Section. To remove the section along with its associated slides, choose the Remove Section & Slides option. To take out all the sections in a presentation, leaving all the slides in place, choose Remove All Sections.

Reuse a Slide from Another Presentation

Suppose you are working on a new presentation and you want to include information covered in an existing presentation. Instead of re-creating the content all over again, you can insert the relevant slide from the existing presentation into the new one.

This is a great timesaver if, for example, you have created a slide with a highly detailed chart, table, or diagram, because it saves you the trouble of reentering data and reformatting the object on the slide. When you insert a slide from a different presentation, the slide automatically adopts the colors, fonts, graphics,

and other formatting attributes of the new presentation (although you can opt to keep the original formatting if you prefer).

To reuse a slide from another presentation, you first locate the presentation containing the slide you want to reuse. This presentation might reside on your computer's hard drive, on a CD you insert in your CD drive, on a network to which your computer is attached, or in a Slide Library on a SharePoint Server. PowerPoint then displays the slides in the selected presentation in the Reuse Slides task pane.

1 In either Normal or Slide Sorter view, select the slide after which you want to insert the new slide.

2 Click the Home tab.

3 Click the New Slide drop-down arrow.

4 Click Reuse Slides.

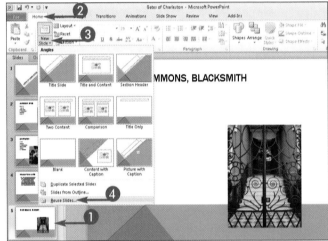

● The Reuse Slides pane opens.

5 Click the Browse button.

6 Click Browse File.

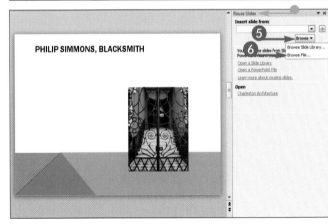

The Browse dialog box opens.

⑦ Navigate to and select the PowerPoint file you want to use.

⑧ Click Open.

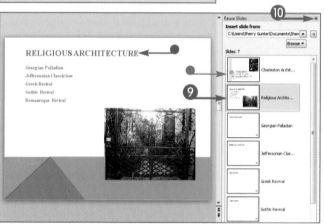

● The presentation's slides are listed in the Reuse Slides pane.

⑨ Click the slide you want to reuse.

● PowerPoint immediately inserts it into the presentation.

⑩ Click the pane's Close button to exit the Reuse Slides pane.

Try This!

To get a better look at the slides in the Reuse Slides task pane, position the mouse pointer over the slide thumbnail rather than the slide title. When you do, an enlarged version of the thumbnail pops up, providing enhanced visibility and readability.

Apply It!

If the slide you are looking for is not in the presentation you selected in the Browse dialog box, click the Browse button in the Reuse Slides task pane and choose Browse File to redisplay the Browse dialog box. Then locate and select the correct presentation file to reveal the presentation's slides in the Reuse Slides task pane.

When delivering a presentation, you typically advance the slides manually by clicking the mouse button. You can, however, set up your presentation to advance the slides automatically. That way, you are free to move as you speak instead of being tethered to your laptop throughout the presentation.

If you opt for automatic slide advancement, you must rehearse the timing of your presentation to ensure that the slides advance at the correct time. To do so, use the Rehearse Timings feature to record the amount of time you need for each slide. PowerPoint then uses the times you record during the presentation

to determine when to advance from one slide to the next.

Note that the Rehearse Timings feature also works well for creating a self-running presentation — that is, a presentation that runs without narration (for example, in a kiosk at a trade show).

As far as slide timing goes, a good rule of thumb is to allow for enough time for your audience to read and view the contents, and if you are speaking along with the presentation, allow enough time to cover all of the necessary points you want to make.

---

① With the slide show you want to rehearse open in PowerPoint, click the Slide Show tab.

② Click Rehearse Timings.

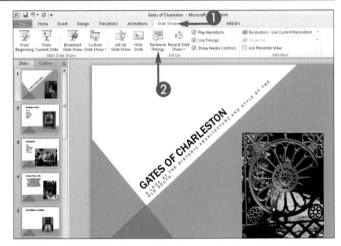

PowerPoint switches to full-screen view and displays the Recording toolbar.

③ Rehearse your speech for the current slide.

● You can click the Pause button to pause the timer at any time.

● The timer for the current slide appears here.

● You can click the Repeat button to restart the timer for the current slide.

● The timer for the overall presentation time appears here.

④ When you are finished speaking or rehearsing with the first slide, click the Next button or the spacebar.

⑤ Repeat steps 3 and 4 for each remaining slide in the presentation.

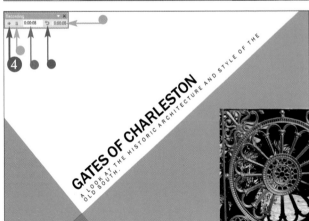

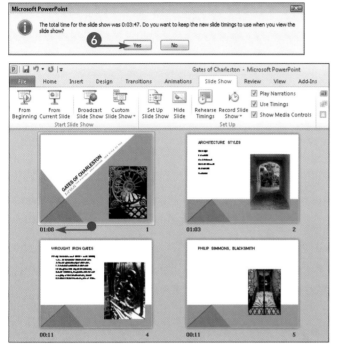

When you click the Next button after rehearsing the last slide, PowerPoint informs you of the total time for the presentation and asks whether you want to keep the new slide timings you created.

⑥ Click Yes if you are satisfied with the slide timings. If you want to change the slide timings, click No and make the desired changes to the presentation.

● PowerPoint displays the slides in the show in Slide Sorter view, with the timing for each slide noted.

Try This!

You can apply transition effects to your PowerPoint presentations. When you do, PowerPoint plays a special effect when advancing from one slide to the next. For example, you can choose a wipe transition effect, where the next slide appears to wipe the current slide from the screen. You can also apply sound effects for transitions, and establish how quickly the transition should occur. You access these settings from the Transitions tab's Transition to This Slide and Timing groups.

More Options!

If you decide you want to advance the slides manually rather than use the timings you set, simply disable the timings by deselecting the Use Timings check box in the Slide Show tab's Set Up group (☑ changes to ☐).

You can use the new Equation Editor to quickly insert common mathematical equations and expressions into your PowerPoint slides. You can also use it to create your own custom equations and expressions. Microsoft's Equation Editor was part of Word 2007 and Excel 2007, but it is now a part of the Office 2010 suite, including PowerPoint. Equation Editor is actually a separate program; it lets you construct equations or expressions without leaving the PowerPoint slide.

You can access the Equation Editor through the Insert tab on the Ribbon. When you activate the Equation Editor, a tab of Equation tools appear on the Ribbon, including operators and symbols, and equation structures.

When you add an equation, PowerPoint creates a text box for the equation on the slide. Like any other slide object you add, you can reposition the text box, resize, and format it.

① Click the Insert tab.

② Click Equation.

● If you click the drop-down arrow, you can choose a preset equation to add.

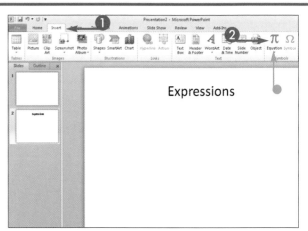

● An equation placeholder text box appears on the slide.

● The Equation Tools Design tab appears on the Ribbon.

③ Type your desired equation.

● You can use the tools on the tab to help you construct your expression or equation.

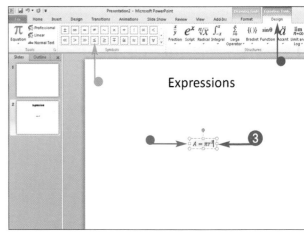

If your presentation is destined for playback at, for example, a booth at a trade show, you can set it up to be a self-running show, with no presenter required. Alternatively, you might burn a self-running presentation to CD and send it to prospective clients. Self-running presentations are perfect in classroom situations, public venues, and as office training modules.

Your self-running presentation can include hyperlinks or action buttons to enable your audience to navigate the presentation;

alternatively, you can set up the show to advance from slide to slide automatically. You can also include voice narration in your self-running presentation. (Follow the steps in the task "Record Narration" earlier in this chapter.) If you want, you can set up your show to *loop* — that is, run over and over again from beginning to end. This is handy if your presentation is running at a trade show booth or kiosk. You set up a presentation to be self-running from the Set Up Show dialog box.

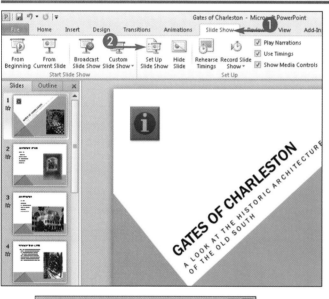

1. With your presentation open, click the Slide Show tab.

2. Click Set Up Slide Show.

The Set Up Show dialog box opens.

3. Click the Browsed at a Kiosk option.

- When you select Browsed at a Kiosk, PowerPoint automatically loops your presentation continuously.

- If you recorded narration for the presentation, make sure the Show Without Narration check box is unchecked.

- If you set timings for your slides, click Using Timings, If Present.

- If you want your viewer to navigate the show manually, click Manually.

4. Click OK.

Write on a Slide During a Presentation

Have you ever given a slide show presentation and wished you could actually write or draw on the slide? You can! PowerPoint lets you draw freehand on your screen during a presentation by turning the mouse into a drawing tool. For example, you might use the highlighter tool to highlight text on a slide, or use the pen tool to annotate an important point or to jot down ideas contributed by your audience. Both tools let you draw or write freehand on the slide.

In addition to writing or highlighting, you can also control the color of your pen or highlighter tool. The color palette lets you pick a color that works best on your slide. For example, a red pen is not easy to view against a red slide background, so you might want to choose another, more visible color instead.

At the end of the presentation you can choose to keep the ink annotations or discard them all.

① While running a presentation, right-click a slide.

② Click Pointer Options.

③ Select a pen type, such as Pen or Highlighter.

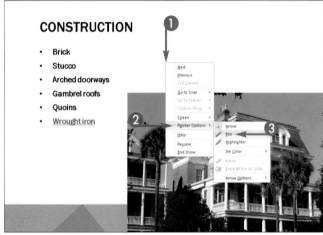

④ Click and drag to draw or write with the pen.

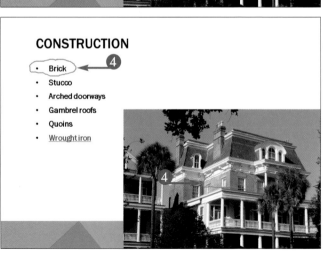

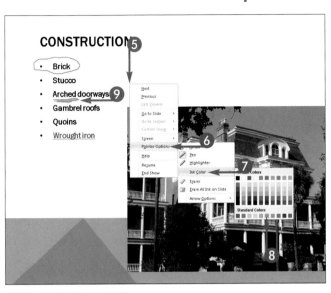

5 To change the pen or highlighter color, right-click the slide again.

6 Click Pointer Options.

7 Click Ink Color.

8 Click a color from the palette.

9 Write on the screen to view the new color.

10 When exiting the presentation, PowerPoint displays a prompt box asking if you want to keep the writing; click Keep to keep your annotations with the presentation, or click Discard to lose them all.

TIPS

Remove It!
To rid a slide of any drawing or writing you have added with the pen or highlighter, simply right-click and click Pointer Options again. To erase only individual elements, choose the Eraser command and then drag over the writing you want to erase. To erase all the writing on a slide, click Erase All Ink on Slide.

More Options!
In addition to a pen or highlighter, you can also turn your mouse pointer into a laser pointer during the slide show. Press and hold Ctrl on the keyboard and then press and hold the mouse pointer. This turns the pointer into a red laser icon. You can also use this technique in Reading view.

When giving a presentation, having a cheat sheet with additional facts, or with answers to questions the audience may ask, is handy. To create just such a cheat sheet, you can enter notes into PowerPoint slides, and then print them out. When you print out the notes you enter, the printout includes a small version of the slide to which the notes refer. You can preview your notes before printing using the Notes Page view.

If you need more room for typing in your slide notes in Normal view, you can resize the Notes pane. Just position your mouse pointer over

the top border of the notes area until the pointer becomes a double-sided arrow pointer (↳ changes to ⬍). Click and drag the border to a taller height to enlarge the notes area.

If you want, you can use PowerPoint's Notes Master to control how printouts of your notes are laid out. For example, you can use the Notes Master to change where the image of the slide appears, as well as to add placeholders for headers, footers, the date, or slide numbers. To use the Notes Master, switch to Notes Master view (click Notes Master in the View tab).

① In Normal view, click a slide in the Slides pane to which you want to add notes.

② Click the Notes pane and type any notes you want to include.

Note: *You can repeat steps 1 and 2 for other slides to which you want to add notes.*

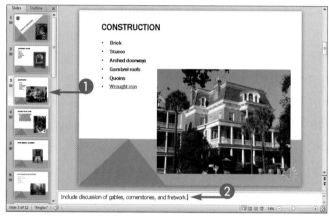

③ Click the View tab.

④ Click Notes Page.

⑤ Click and drag the Zoom bar to zoom in and see your note text for each slide.

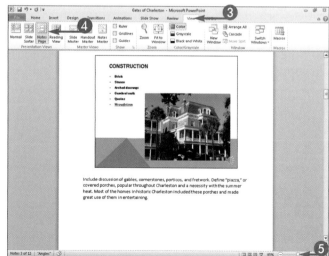

To help your audience follow along as you perform your presentation, as well as provide a place for them to take notes for future reference, you can print presentation handouts. These handouts can contain one, three, five, six, or nine slides per page. (Printing several slides per page can help you save paper when printing handouts for a lengthy presentation.)

When selecting handout orientation, you can choose Horizontal or Vertical to indicate how the slides should be oriented on the printout. Choosing Vertical prints slides in order down the left column, continuing in order down the right column.

You can use PowerPoint's Handout Master to control how your presentation handouts are laid out. For example, you can use the Handout Master to change where the images of the slides appear, as well as add placeholders for headers, footers, the date, slide numbers, a company logo, and so on. To use the Handout Master, switch to Handout Master view (click Handout Master in the View tab). Then use the various tools available on the Handout Master tab to add or remove placeholders, change the fonts or colors used, and so on.

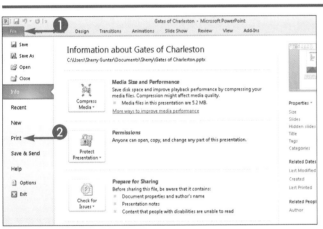

① Click the File tab.

② Click Print.

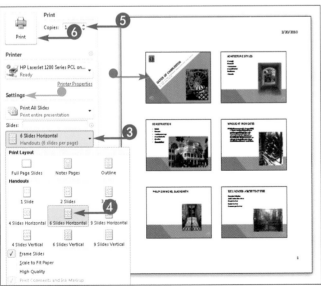

● Backstage view displays the Print settings.

③ Under Settings, click here.

④ Click the number of slides that should appear on each page.

● The preview area shows what the printed page will look like.

⑤ Specify how many copies you want to print.

⑥ Click Print.

PowerPoint prints the handouts.

Compress Media Files

If your presentation includes a lot of embedded media files, such as soundtracks, narration, video and movie clips, you may end up with a presentation that consumes a great deal of file space. Media clips are notorious consumers of file size. Thankfully, PowerPoint 2010 offers a tool to help you save disk space. You can compress your media files and even improve playback quality.

The Compress Media feature keeps track of your overall file size, and you can view this notation using the Info tab in Backstage view. You can choose from three quality settings: Presentation Quality, Internet Quality, and

Low Quality. Choose Presentation Quality if you want to maintain high quality yet save some space. Choose Internet Quality to emulate streaming media found on the Internet. Choose Low Quality if you are sending the presentation as a file attachment.

After the compression process is completed, the Info screen displays information about what quality setting you applied. If the compression results were not to your liking, you can click the Compress Media button and choose Undo, and then try another quality setting.

---

① Click the File tab.

② Click Info.

● Overall media space consumption is listed here.

③ Click Compress Media.

④ Click a quality setting.

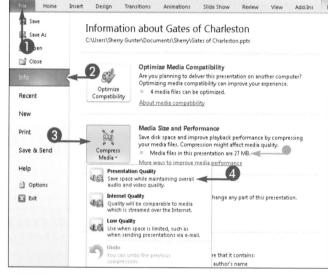

● The Compress Media dialog box appears and displays compression progress.

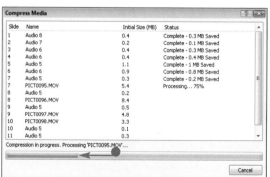

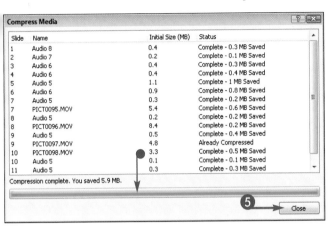

- When the compression is complete, view how much disk space you have saved here.

⑤ Click Close.

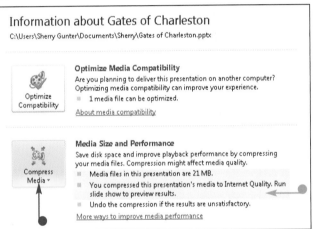

- The Media Size and Performance area lists the type of compression you used.

- Click Compress Media and click Undo if you want to undo the compression.

TIPS

More Options!

If your presentation is full of digital images instead of media files, you can use PowerPoint's Compress Pictures option to help cut down on file size. Select a picture in a slide to display the Picture Tools Format tab, and then click the Compress Pictures button. The Compress Pictures dialog box opens and you can choose a compression option and a target output. For example, you can discard cropped areas of your pictures to save space, and optimize the pictures for e-mailing or printing.

More Options!

You can also use the Optimize Media Compatibility feature to help ensure your files play back properly on other computers. To bypass problems encountered by end users who are unable to play your media clips properly because of missing decoders, activate the Optimize Media Compatibility feature. Click the File tab, click Info, and then click Optimize Compatibility.

Turn a Presentation into a Video

PowerPoint has always offered users a variety of ways to share their presentations, such as sending them via e-mail, uploading them onto the Internet, or packaging them onto CDs for distribution. With PowerPoint 2010, you can now turn your slide show into a video.

Previously you had to use a special program to accomplish such a conversion. Most people have access to video players today, including through such devices as iPods and iPhones. You can easily turn your presentation into a Windows media video file (WMV). If you want to use another file format, you need a third-party utility to do so.

Using the Create Video feature, you can turn your presentation into a video file that includes all of your assigned transitions, narration, slide timings, and animations. You can choose from three quality settings ranging from larger to smaller in overall file size. Choose Computer & HD Displays to maintain the highest quality setting appropriate for monitors, projectors, or high definition television. Choose Internet & DVD quality if you plan to save the file to a DVD or the Internet. To prepare the presentation for a mobile device, choose the Portable Devices setting.

---

① Click the File tab.

② Click Save & Send.

③ Click Create a Video.

④ Click here and choose a quality setting.

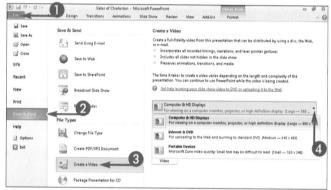

⑤ Click here and choose whether you want to include recorded timings and narrations or not.

Note: By default, PowerPoint assigns a five second default time to slides without preset timings; you can change the timing here to increase or decrease the time.

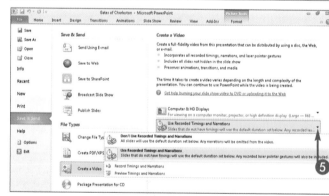

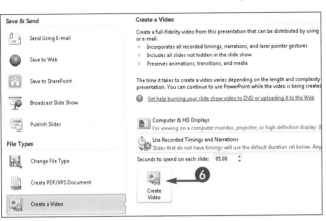

⑥ Click Create Video.

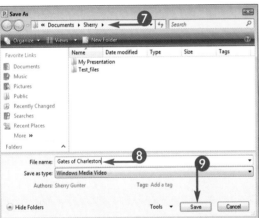

The Save As dialog box appears.

⑦ Navigate to the folder or drive where you want to store the file.

⑧ Type a name for the file.

⑨ Click Save.

PowerPoint creates the video file.

Note: *Depending on your presentation, the conversion process for turning a slide show into a video file can take several hours. You may prefer to set this process up to occur overnight so the video file is done and ready for use in the morning.*

Note: *To play a video, navigate to the folder where you saved the file and double-click the file name.*

More Options!

You may prefer to save your presentation to a DVD so that anyone with a standard DVD or disc player can watch it. Start by saving the presentation as a video file as outlined in this task. Then open Windows DVD Maker, click Add Items, and select your newly created video file. Click the Add button, choose your burner, pop in a DVD, and burn the file to the disc. Windows DVD Maker is included in Windows Vista Home Premium and Windows 7 (Home Premium, Professional, and Ultimate editions).

Did You Know?

Just what parts of a presentation are not included in a video file? PowerPoint does not include any media clips you inserted into your slides from previous PowerPoint versions. Any QuickTime media clips are not included, no macros are included, and no OLE or ActiveX controls are stored either. Items definitely included are sounds, narration, animations, transitions, and slide timings.

Broadcast a Presentation

New to PowerPoint 2010, you can broadcast a presentation to multiple participants. Similar to a live meeting broadcast, you can use the PowerPoint Broadcast Service to present a slide show, live and synchronized, to friends or colleagues regardless of their location. Simply send them a link provided by the feature and start the show when you are ready to present it. Best of all, the invitees do not need to have PowerPoint 2010 installed in order to view the show. They can use their default browsers to view the presentation.

You need a Windows Live account in order to use this service. If you are not logged on, you need to sign in first to use the service. If you do not have a Windows Live account, use your browser to navigate to www.home.live.com and follow the instructions for creating an account.

When you send out a link to recipients, they can share the link with others. Because the link is public, anyone with the link can view the show.

---

① Click the File tab.

② Click Save & Send.

③ Click Broadcast Slide Show.

④ Click Broadcast Slide Show.

Note: *You can also click the Broadcast Slide Show button on the Slide Show tab to start the process.*

The Broadcast Slide Show dialog box appears.

⑤ Click Start Broadcast.

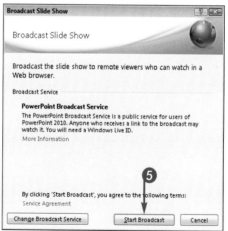

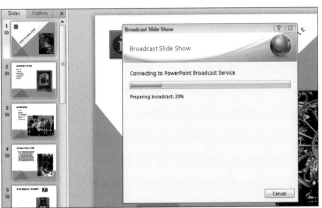

PowerPoint connects you to the broadcast service and prepares your presentation.

Note: *If you are not already logged onto your Windows Live account, you are prompted to do so before preparing the presentation.*

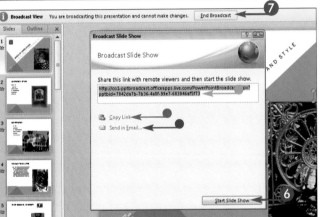

● When you are ready to give the presentation, share the link shown here with your friends or colleagues.

● Click here if you want to copy the link.

● You can click here to send the link in an e-mail.

⑥ When you are ready to start the show, click Start Slide Show.

⑦ When finished, click End Broadcast.

TIP

More Options!

If you are a SharePoint user, you can also save your PowerPoint presentation to a SharePoint site, which allows you to collaborate with others in your workgroup. SharePoint uses the same broadcasting tools described in this task to upload a presentation file to a designated spot on the Web. To save your presentation to a SharePoint site, click the File tab, click Save & Send, and then click the Save to SharePoint option. You can browse for a location, and then click Save As to start the process.

Enhancing Your Presentations

Whatever your presentation's message, PowerPoint is designed to enable you to convey it in the most interesting way possible. To that end, the program offers countless features for enhancing your presentation visually.

When you create a presentation, PowerPoint enables you to select from several predesigned slide layouts. A slide's layout determines how the title, text, graphics, and other visual elements are positioned in a slide. You are not compelled to use existing layouts all the time. You can create your own custom layouts and save them to reuse in other presentations.

In addition to selecting the slide layout, you can apply themes to your slides. A theme is a set of colors, fonts, placeholder positions, graphic elements, backgrounds, effects, and other formatting attributes. PowerPoint installs with a variety of premade themes

that help you to streamline the look and feel of your presentation. You can also customize an existing theme, as well as save the custom work as a new theme to add to the library.

Of course, you are not limited to including text-based content in your slides. PowerPoint enables you to insert any number of objects, such as images, video, sound, and SmartArt graphics. Introduced in Office 2007, SmartArt graphics are ideal for creating organizational charts and illustrating other concepts and processes. In Office 2010, Microsoft has added more graphics to the library.

For added interest, you can animate slide objects — for example, you might set up your slide show to fly in an image from the upper left portion of the screen, landing it in the bottom right corner. In moderate doses, animation can go a long way toward keeping your audience engaged.

Quick Steps

PowerPoint installs with a myriad of layouts; however, if none of the standard layouts available in PowerPoint's Layout gallery quite suits your needs, you can create a new layout from scratch. You create a new layout from within Slide Master view and give it a unique name. (You can learn more about this view in the next task.) When you create a new layout, you add the necessary text- and object-specific placeholders.

Whether working with a predefined layout or a custom one, you can edit the placeholders in a slide's layout. For example, you can resize a placeholder, move it to another location on your slide, or delete it entirely. You can also add as many placeholders to a slide as you need. You can determine exactly what kind of placeholder to add, such as a text box, clip art, chart, or multimedia item. Anytime you add a placeholder element, you can control the size for the content it holds just by defining its dimensions by "drawing" the placeholder on the slide. To do this, you drag the placeholder box to the size you want when inserting the item.

After you have created your custom layout, PowerPoint adds it to the Layout gallery, and you can reuse it throughout your presentation. You can also save the entire presentation as a template to make the custom layout available in new presentations you create using the template.

① Click the View tab.

② Click Slide Master.

● The Slide Master tab appears in the Ribbon and is selected by default.

③ Click Insert Layout.

● PowerPoint adds a new default slide to the list.

④ Customize the layout as needed.

● Remove any unwanted default placeholders by clicking the border or bounding box of the placeholder and pressing Delete on your keyboard.

Note: *To move a placeholder, position your mouse pointer over the placeholder's bounding box (that is, the box surrounding the placeholder). The mouse pointer changes to a four-headed arrow ( ); click and drag to relocate the placeholder.*

● To add a placeholder, click the Insert Placeholder drop-down arrow, click the type of placeholder you want to insert, and then drag to draw the placeholder in the slide.

⑤ Click Rename.

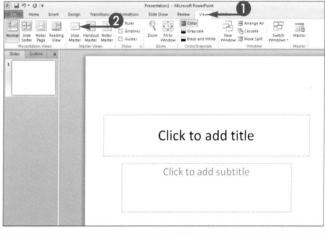

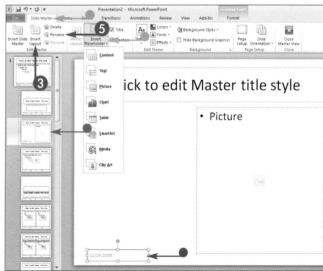

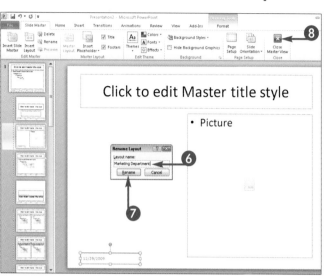

The Rename Layout dialog box opens.

⑥ Type a unique name for the layout.

⑦ Click Rename.

⑧ Click Close Master View.

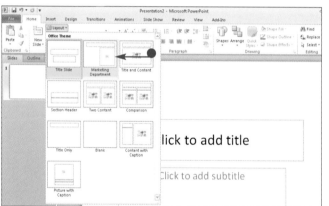

● The new layout is now listed in the New Slide and Layout galleries.

Try This!

To resize a placeholder, first click in the placeholder, and then position your mouse pointer over a sizing handle on the placeholder. The mouse pointer changes to a two-headed arrow (✕); click and drag inward or outward to change the size of the placeholder. (Note: To preserve the aspect ratio of the placeholder — that is, the ratio of the height and width — press and hold Shift and drag one of the corner-sizing handles.)

Apply It!

To save a presentation as a template, simply select PowerPoint Template from the Save As Type drop-down menu in the Save As dialog box (click the File tab and click Save As). You can apply the template as a new presentation at any time by clicking the File tab, New, and selecting the template file from the My Templates folder.

Insert a Custom Slide Master

You can insert your own custom slide masters into a PowerPoint presentation. By definition, a *slide master* determines the type of content and positioning of the various placeholders in the slide. Much like a template for controlling a Word document, a PowerPoint slide master is a template upon which all the presentation's slides are based — a pattern, if you will, for all the slides you add to the presentation. Slide masters are a great way to save time formatting and create a unifying look for a long presentation. It makes sure any additional slides you add always share the same look and feel.

You can customize a slide master to suit your presentation needs. Each slide master you add includes a subset of corresponding layouts. When you apply a theme to a presentation, that theme includes predefined slide masters. If you make a change to a slide master, such as increasing the font size for slide titles or adding a footer or graphic, that change is applied to every slide in the presentation.

You work with the slide master in Slide Master view. You can use the specialized tools on this Ribbon tab to delete, create, preserve, or rename masters, or change the placeholders contained in the master layout.

① With the presentation for which you want to create a custom slide master open in PowerPoint, click the View tab.

② Click Slide Master.

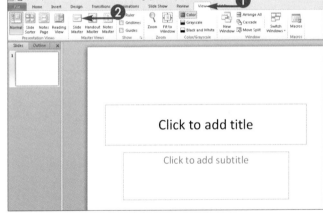

The Slide Master tab appears in the Ribbon and is selected by default.

③ Click Insert Slide Master.

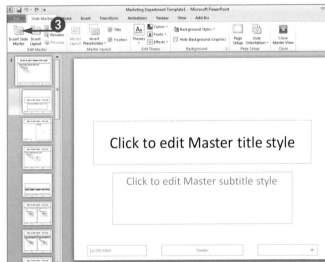

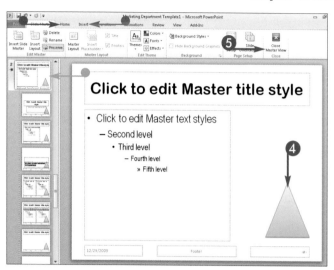

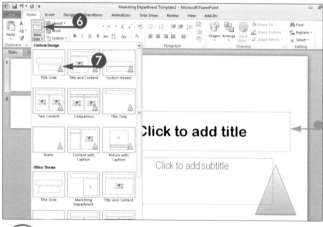

- A new slide master appears along with a subset of layouts.

④ Edit the slide master as needed.

- You can use the Insert tab to insert elements such as footers, a date, slide numbers, graphics, or what have you.

- You can use the Home tab to apply formatting to the various slide elements.

⑤ When you finish customizing the new slide master, click the Close Master View button on the Slide Master tab.

Note: Be sure to save the presentation as a template file to use the custom slide master in other presentations you create.

⑥ To apply a slide using the new slide master, click the New Slide button on the Home tab.

⑦ Click a slide.

- PowerPoint displays a slide based on the new slide master.

TIPS

Try This!

In addition to inserting footers, images, and other items into slide masters, you can also insert placeholders. A placeholder reserves space in a slide for a particular type of element, such as a picture. You can then replace the placeholder with the specific picture you want to use. In this way, you can use a different picture on each slide, even though the same master is applied. To insert a placeholder, click the Slide Master tab, click Insert Placeholder, and choose the type of placeholder you want to insert.

Did You Know?

PowerPoint uses four different master slides for your presentations. As you have already learned, the Slide Master is the boss of all the other slides you add to your presentation, with the exception of the Title Master. The Title Slide Master is the layout template for the Title page only. The Notes Master and Handout Master control Notes pages and Handout pages. You can create a custom master for each type.

Streamline Your Presentation with Themes

Although you can manually format the slides in your presentation one by one — applying backgrounds, fonts, colors, graphics, and so on — an easier way to streamline the look and feel of the slides in your presentation is to apply a theme. Doing so applies specific colors, fonts, placeholder positions, graphic elements, backgrounds, effects, and other formatting to the slides in the presentation in one quick, easy operation. PowerPoint installs with a large library of ready-to-go themes you can apply. The theme's slide masters determine the

positioning of the placeholders and objects for the current theme, saving you time and effort doing it all yourself.

You can apply one theme to all the slides in a presentation to lend a consistent, professional look. Alternatively, you can apply different themes to certain slides. Note that if you do opt to apply a different theme to certain slides, be sure it complements the design used on other slides. Otherwise, the transition from one theme to another as you move from slide to slide can be jarring to viewers.

① With the presentation to which you want to apply a theme open in PowerPoint, click the Design tab.

② Click the More button to display the Themes gallery.

③ Move your mouse pointer to a theme thumbnail.

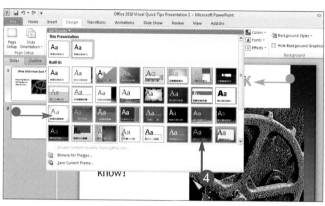

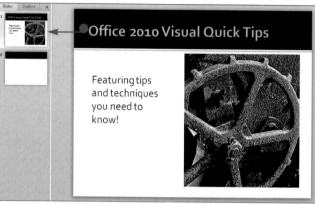

● With Live Preview, you can preview any design theme you position the mouse pointer over in the Slide pane.

● Theme thumbnails display their associated color palettes along with the applied theme formatting.

❹ When you find a theme you want to apply, click its thumbnail.

● PowerPoint applies the theme to all the slides in the presentation.

Did You Know?

Generally, dark-colored backgrounds with light-colored text work better in darker spaces, such as hotel conference rooms. Lighter backgrounds are easier to read in brighter, smaller spaces, such as small meeting rooms. Be warned: People may grow weary of looking at bright colors such as oranges or reds for an extended period of time.

Try This!

As mentioned, you can apply different themes to certain slides. To do so, switch to Slide Sorter view and select the slides to which you want to apply the different theme. (Press and hold Ctrl as you click to select noncontiguous slides in the presentation.) Then open the Themes gallery, right-click the theme you want to apply to the selected slides, and choose Apply to Selected Slides.

If you apply a theme to your presentation, but decide that you would prefer to use different colors or fonts with that theme, you can easily change them by selecting a different color theme or font theme. A *color theme* controls the colors automatically applied to text and objects such as tables and SmartArt diagrams. The *font theme* dictates the font formatting for all text.

Changing the color theme or font theme can give your presentation an entirely fresh look, even as other theme attributes are retained.

Choosing different color and font themes can also help make your presentation more attractive — not to mention readable — when it appears on-screen or in printout form.

In addition to applying a new predefined color theme or font theme to your presentation, you can also create your own custom color and font themes.

You can apply a different color theme to selected slides in your presentation or to the entire show. The font theme, however, must be applied to the presentation in its entirety.

Apply a New Color Theme

1. With the presentation whose theme you want to change open in PowerPoint, click the Design tab.

2. Click Colors.

- A gallery of color themes appears.

3. Choose the color theme you want to apply.

- PowerPoint applies the color theme.

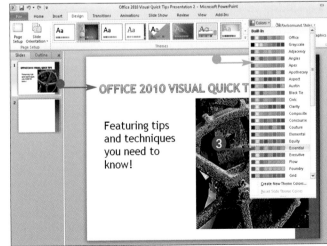

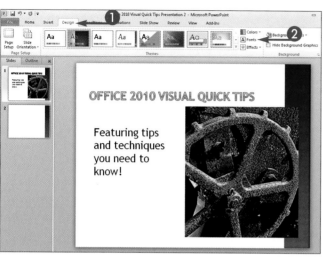

Apply a New Font Theme

① With the presentation whose theme you want to change open in PowerPoint, click the Design tab.

② Click Fonts.

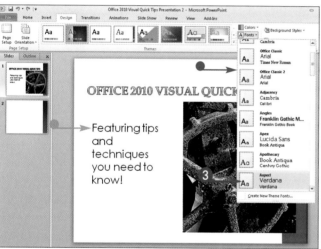

● A gallery of font themes appears.

③ Choose the font theme you want to apply.

● PowerPoint applies the font theme you chose.

Try This!

You can create your own custom color theme or font theme by clicking Colors or Fonts and clicking Create New Theme Colors/Create New Theme Fonts. In the dialog box that appears, select the desired colors or font, type a name for the custom color or font theme, and click Save. You can then apply the custom color or font theme just as you would a built-in one.

More Options!

You may have more themes available in other places on your computer. Click the More button in the Themes group to display the full gallery, and then click the Browse for Themes command. You can browse for themes on your own computer using the Choose Theme or Themed Document dialog box. You can also check Microsoft's Office Web site for more themes you can download and use with PowerPoint.

If you opt to apply formatting to your slides manually, or if you customize an existing theme, you can save your formatting choices as a new theme. Doing so enables you to apply the same formatting settings to other presentations in the same way you would apply any other theme.

If you want, you can make the theme you save — or any other theme, for that matter — the default theme. PowerPoint then automatically applies that theme to any

new presentations you create. To make a theme the default theme, click the Design tab, click the More button, right-click the theme you want to set as the default, and choose Set as Default Theme.

In addition to saving themes you create for reuse, you can save presentations you create as templates on which subsequent presentations can be based. The template file includes both the presentation design (that is, the theme) and content, such as bulleted lists.

① With the presentation whose theme you want to save open in PowerPoint, click the Design tab.

② Click the More button to display the Themes gallery.

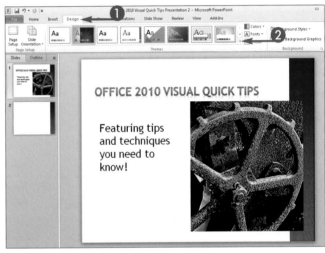

③ Click Save Current Theme.

The Save Current Theme dialog box appears.

④ Type a file name.

Note: Do not change the folder in which the theme is saved. Using the default location ensures that the custom theme appears in the Themes gallery.

⑤ Click Save.

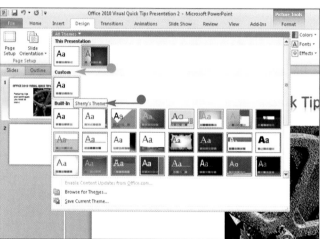

● PowerPoint adds the theme to the gallery in a special section labeled Custom.

● You can position your mouse pointer over a thumbnail to reveal its name.

More Options!

You can share your themes with others. Themes are saved in the Document Themes folder by default as .thmx file types. You can copy and share the theme files with other users who can store them in their own Document Themes folder or locate the shared theme through the Browse for Themes command (click the Themes group More button and then click Browse for Themes).

Try This!

In addition to saving themes you create, you can also save a presentation as a template. To save a presentation as a template, click the File tab, click Save As, type a name for the template, click the Save As Type drop-down arrow, choose PowerPoint Template, and click Save.

Adding graphic elements, such as clip art or your own personal photos or other images (for example, a company logo) can enhance the slide's appearance and give it some visual impact. This is especially helpful because most people are typically visually oriented by nature. Graphic elements can be placed anywhere on your slide.

After you insert a picture into your slide, you can move and resize it as needed. To move a picture, click it in the slide, rest your mouse pointer over the box surrounding it, click, and drag it to the desired location. Resize a picture by clicking it, and then clicking and dragging

any of the resizing handles that appear around the border of the picture. Depending on the picture type, you can also rotate and flip pictures. To rotate a picture, click the object to select it, and then drag its rotation handle, the green circle located at the top middle of the picture.

To otherwise edit a picture — for example, to change the image's brightness, contrast, or color tone, crop it, apply a picture style, add a border, and so on — click the picture to select it, click the Format tab, and use any of the various tools that appear.

Insert Clip Art

1. With the slide to which you want to add clip art open in Normal view, click the Insert tab.

2. Click Clip Art.

   The Clip Art task pane appears.

3. Type a search keyword or phrase.

   ● Click here and select what type of files you want your search to return.

4. Click Go.

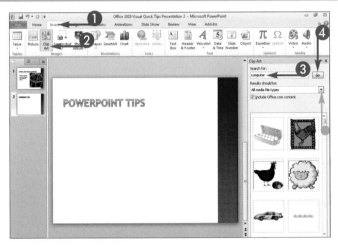

   ● The Clip Art task pane displays any matching search results.

   ● Scroll to locate the picture you want.

5. Click the picture.

   ● PowerPoint inserts it into the slide. You can move or resize the clip art as needed.

6. Click to close the Clip Art task pane.

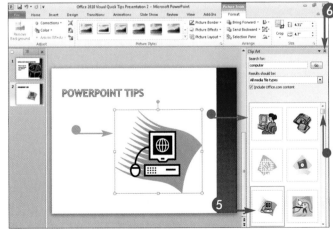

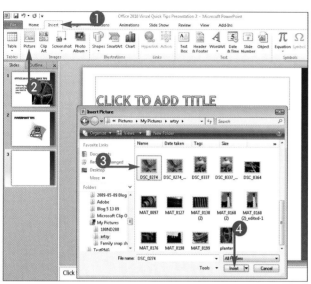

Insert a Picture

1. With the slide to which you want to add a picture open in Normal view, click the Insert tab.

2. Click Picture.

   The Insert Picture dialog box opens.

3. Navigate to and select the picture file you want to insert.

4. Click Insert.

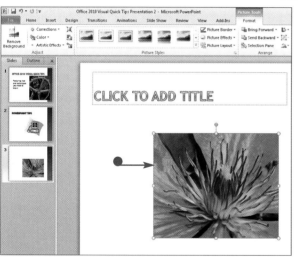

● PowerPoint inserts the image. You can resize or move the picture as needed.

Did You Know?
To find all kinds of formatting options for your picture or clip art graphic, just open the Format Picture dialog box. Right-click the graphic object and click Format Picture. In the Format Picture dialog box, you can find commands listed under a variety of tabs, such as Picture Corrections, Artistic Effects, and Position.

Try This!
You can double-click a clip art object or picture to quickly bring the Picture Tools Format tab in view on the Ribbon, offering you all kinds of commands for formatting the graphic.

Insert a SmartArt Graphic

You can insert a SmartArt graphic or diagram to illustrate a process, hierarchy, cycle, or relationship. For example, a diagram can show the workflow in a procedure or the hierarchy in an organization, as illustrated in this task. Using SmartArt graphics, you can create designer-quality graphics that beautifully convey your message with a few clicks of the mouse. PowerPoint offers dozens of SmartArt graphic layouts. Simply insert the graphic you want to use and add any necessary text.

When you insert a SmartArt graphic into your presentation, it has the same visual characteristics (that is, the color, style, and so on) of other content in the presentation. You can, however, change the style or color of the SmartArt graphic, or add effects such as glow or 3-D. You can even animate your SmartArt graphic. To remove any formatting changes you make to a SmartArt graphic, click the Design tab and click Reset Graphic.

You can also find the SmartArt feature in Word and Excel.

① Click the Insert tab.

② Click SmartArt.

If your slide layout has a content placeholder, you can click the Insert SmartArt Graphic icon instead.

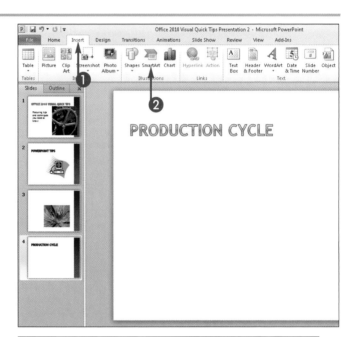

The Choose a SmartArt Graphic dialog box appears.

③ Click a diagram style.

④ Click a specific diagram layout.

⑤ Click OK.

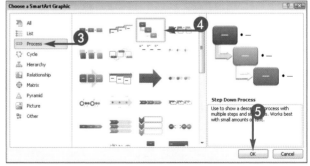

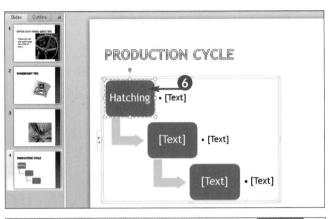

The dialog box closes and the diagram appears on the slide, ready for editing.

6 Click in a shape in the diagram and type the desired text.

● To add more shapes to the diagram, click the shape and click Add Shape, choosing where the new shape should appear.

● Click an option in the Layouts group to change the layout of the SmartArt graphic.

● Click Change Colors to choose a different set of colors for the SmartArt diagram.

● Choose a new style for the SmartArt graphic from the SmartArt Styles group.

7 Repeat step 6 for the remaining diagram elements.

8 Click outside the diagram to finish creating it.

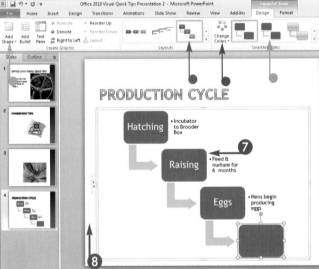

Did You Know?

PowerPoint automatically resizes the text you type to fit the SmartArt diagram. You do not need to adjust the font size yourself. The more text you type, the smaller it is. You can apply formatting to any of the SmartArt text; select it and position the mouse pointer over the mini toolbar and select from the formatting controls, or use the formatting controls on the Home tab or on the SmartArt Tools tabs.

Try This!

If your slide already contains the text you want to appear in your SmartArt graphic, you can convert it. To do so, click in the placeholder that contains the text you want to convert to a SmartArt graphic. Then click the Home tab and, in the Paragraph group, click Convert to SmartArt Graphic. (Alternatively, right-click the placeholder that contains the text you want to convert and choose Convert to SmartArt.) A gallery of SmartArt graphic layouts appears; click the one you want to use.

Add Video or Sound to Your Presentation

To enhance your presentation, you can add video or movie clips to it. For example, if you have composed a presentation for an alumni association meeting, you might include a clip showing the campus. You can set up PowerPoint to play back your video automatically; alternatively, you can choose to play it manually by clicking it. Supported video file formats include AVI (Audio Video Interleave), MPEG (Moving Picture Experts Group), and WMV (Windows Media Video).

Video files are always linked to, rather than embedded in, PowerPoint presentations to reduce the size of the presentation file. For this reason, it is wise to first copy the video file into

the same folder in which your PowerPoint presentation is stored; this ensures that your presentation can locate the file when necessary.

You can also insert sound clips into your presentation. When you do, PowerPoint adds a small speaker icon to the selected slide. When you position the mouse pointer over the speaker icon, a player control bar appears with buttons for playing the clip. (If the speaker icon clashes with your slide design, and if you have set up the sound to play automatically, you can hide the speaker icon by clicking it, clicking the Playback tab, and selecting the Hide During Show check box.)

Insert a Video Clip

1. Click the Insert tab.

2. Click the Video arrow.

3. Choose Video from File.

   The Insert Video dialog box appears.

4. Select the video file you want to insert.

5. Click Insert.

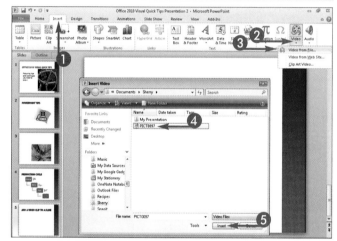

- The clip is added to the slide. You can move or resize the clip, as needed.

- Point to the clip and click to play the clip.

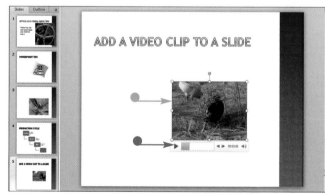

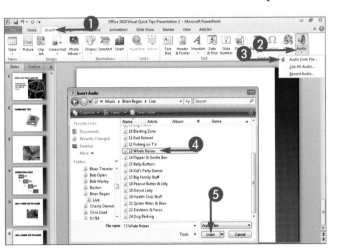

Insert a Sound Clip

1 Click the Insert tab.

2 Click the Audio arrow.

3 Choose Audio from File.

The Insert Audio dialog box appears.

4 Select the audio file you want to insert.

5 Click Insert.

● The clip is added to the slide as a speaker icon. You can move or resize the speaker icon, as needed.

● Point to the icon and click to play the clip.

ADD A SOUND CLIP TO A SLIDE

More Options!

You can control how a video clip or sound clip plays in a movie using the settings found on the Playback tab (Audio Tools) or the Playback tab (Video Tools), one of the two special tabs that appear when you select the clip in the slide. You can use the Start setting to specify whether the clip plays when clicked or automatically. You can also loop the clip to play continuously or rewind when finished playing.

More Options!

If you want to look for media clips to insert, instead of inserting a clip of your own, click the Video arrow in the Insert tab and choose Clip Art Video. The Clip Art task pane opens; type a keyword describing the type of clip you want to find and click Go. To preview a clip, position your mouse pointer over it, click the down arrow that appears, and choose Preview/Properties.

By default, items you add to your slides remain static. To add interest, you can animate the items on PowerPoint slides — that is, apply motion to the text or objects in your slide, such as images, bulleted lists, and the like. For example, you might animate a table on your slide to move in from the top of the screen.

The Ribbon's Animations tab contains options for setting up and working with animations in your presentation. You simply select the item in your presentation you want to animate, and

then choose the desired animation effect from the tab. PowerPoint previews the animation for you right after you apply it. Another option is to create a custom animation, as outlined here.

Be warned: You should avoid overusing animations. Otherwise, your presentation may seem too busy. Excessive use of animations can overshadow the message of your presentation. By using animations sparingly, you ensure they serve as effective attention grabbers rather than distractions.

① Click the object you want to animate to select it.

② Click the Animations tab.

③ Click the Animation gallery's More button.

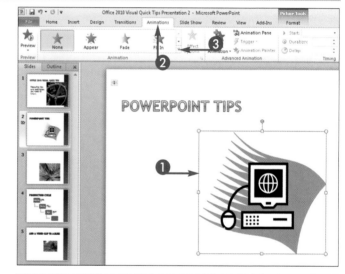

④ Click an effect.

● As you peruse the effects and position the mouse pointer over an animation, PowerPoint's Live Preview feature demonstrates the effect on the selected object in the Slide pane.

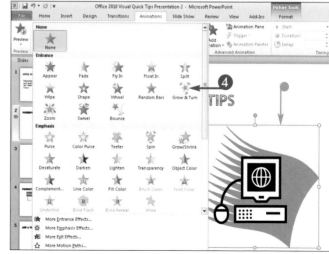

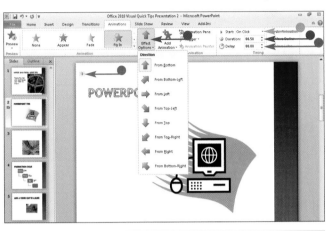

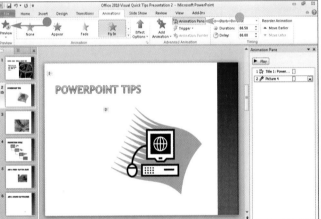

- PowerPoint displays a tiny number icon next to each animation you assign to a slide element.

- If the animation has a directional control, click Effect Options and set the desired direction or path.

- Click here and choose an option for starting the animation.

- Click here and choose a duration for the effect.

- Click here to set a delay time.

- If assigning more than one animation to a slide, click the Animation pane to view a list of effects. You can use the pane to reorder the effects or make changes to their status.

- To preview the effect again, click the Preview button.

Note: To remove an animation effect, select the object, click the More button in the Animation gallery, and click None. You can also click the effect's drop-down arrow in the Animation pane and click Remove.

Try This!
You can apply multiple animations to an object. If you do, you can then specify the order in which the animations should occur. To change the order, click an animation you want to move in the Animation pane and then click the up and down arrow buttons along the bottom of the pane to move it up or down, respectively.

Did You Know?
If you select a complex object — for example, a SmartArt diagram — you can apply animation to each of its individual parts. Simply select the part you want to animate and apply the animation as normal.

Read Less-Learn More®

Want instruction in other topics?

Check out these

All designed for visual learners—just like you!

Teach Yourself **VISUALLY**
Mac
OS X Lion
The Fast and Easy Way to Learn

Paul McFedries

978-1-118-02241-2

Teach Yourself **VISUALLY**
HTML5
The Fast and Easy Way to Learn

Mike Wooldridge

978-1-1180-6332-3

Read Less-Learn More®
Teach Yourself **VISUALLY**
Digital Photography
4th Edition

The Fast
and Easy Way
to Learn

Chris Bucher

978-0-470-58946-5

Available in print and e-book formats.

**For a complete listing of *Teach Yourself VISUALLY*™ titles
and other Visual books, go to wiley.com/go/visual**

Visual
An Imprint of ⊕WILEY